THE LOW AMBITION HANDBOOK

WARNING While every effort has been made to include sound tips and guidance in this book, the publisher, authors and their associates, including experts and colleagues who have offered advice, cannot guarantee that the information contained herein is acccurate, complete or safe, and disclaim all liability from any injury or financial loss that may result from its use.

THE
LOW AMBITION HANDBOOK

Nicola Chalton & Pascal Thivillon

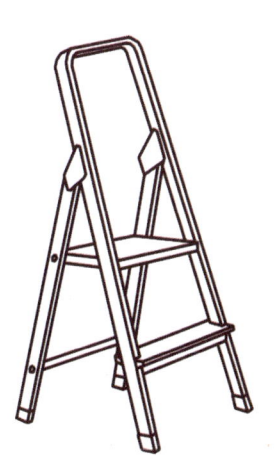

BASEMENT PRESS
London

★

A Basement Press Book
www.basementpress.com

This edition published by Basement Press
in conjunction with Worth Press Ltd

First published in the UK by Ottakar's Plc
in 2004

Copyright © 2004 Nicola Chalton & Pascal Thivillon

All rights reserved.
This book is sold subject to the condition that
it shall not, by way of trade or otherwise, be lent, re-sold, hired out
or otherwise circulated in any form of binding or cover other than
that in which it is published and without a similar condition including
this condition being imposed on the subsequent purchaser

A copy of the British Library Cataloguing in Publication Data
is available from the British Library

ISBN 0-9548361-0-3

Printed and bound in the EU

10 9 8 7 6 5 4 3 2 1

★

CONTENTS

★

vii **Introduction**

1 **Week 1**
Making a bed
with hospital corners

5 **Week 2**
Deciphering a utility bill

8 **Week 3**
Changing a light bulb

12 **Week 4**
Getting the right tone
on an answering machine

15 **Week 5**
Making toast

18 **Week 6**
Keeping a fish in a fish bowl

22 **Week 7**
Giving a massage

25 **Week 8**
Deterring a burglar

29 **Week 9**
Disguising a lack
of knowledge

32 **Week 10**
Building a snowdome
collection

36 **Week 11**
Removing cat hairs
from a suit

39 **Week 12**
Cleaning a chandelier

43 **Week 13**
Coping with a hangover

46 **Week 14**
Plugging in a video

49 **Week 15**
Mending a flat bicycle tyre

53 **Week 16**
Making a space rocket mobile

57 **Week 17**
Removing a slug infestation

61 **Week 18**
Keeping socks in pairs

64 **Week 19**
Mowing a lawn

67 **Week 20**
Choosing a tie

71 **Week 21**
Removing a spider

74 **Week 22**
Unplugging a clogged sink

78 **Week 23**
Lighting a barbecue

81 **Week 24**
Planting a tub of mustard
and cress

84 **Week 25**
Rolling up a sleeping bag

87 **Week 26**
Complaining to
the council

90 **Week 27**
Opening a tin can

94 **Week 28**
Ironing a frilly blouse

97 **Week 29**
Feeding a hedgehog

101 **Week 30**
Putting up a deckchair

105 **Week 31**
Ending an affair

108 **Week 32**
Removing a splinter

111 **Week 33**
Erecting a three-man tent

114 **Week 34**
Taking a siesta

118 **Week 35**
Preparing for
a chemical attack

122 **Week 36**
Putting up a hem

126 **Week 37**
Avoiding hooligans

129 **Week 38**
Applying nail varnish
to toes

132 **Week 39**
Cleaning a toilet bowl

136 **Week 40**
Looking after
a nylon stocking

140 **Week 41**
Making a rockery
on a window sill

143 **Week 42**
Hanging a patterned
wallcovering

147 **Week 43**
Dealing with facial hair

150 **Week 44**
Changing a nappy

154 **Week 45**
Sharpening a carving knife

158 **Week 46**
Shampooing a dog

162 **Week 47**
Making friends
in the office

166 **Week 48**
Deodorizing
a refrigerator

169 **Week 49**
Making a paper aeroplane

173 **Week 50**
Mending a fuse in the dark

177 **Week 51**
Preserving a
Christmas tree

180 **Week 52**
Getting guests to go home

183 **About the authors**

184 **Acknowledgements**

INTRODUCTION

★

'Everyone is trying to accomplish something big,
not realizing that life is made up of little things.'
Frank A. Clark

Yesterday we saw a man deflecting bullets in a superhuman reflex. The day before that, a woman with her baby surviving a helicopter jump and escaping killer sharks. The day before that, a junior doctor brilliantly saving a kidney failure victim under emergency dialysis. And – in the afternoon – a stunning, not-guilty verdict secured by an impossibly handsome barrister for an impossibly beautiful, but obviously guilty, accused. Courtroom dramas, hospital soaps, action-hero adventures flood our TV and cinema screens, books and gaming software with unlikely scenarios.

Then there's ambition – that desire for success, wealth or fame which invaded our waking consciousness from the moment we could write 'comic book hero' in an exercise book, and to which we have slavishly devoted our lives. But for what? Apparently, no good reason. Judging by the celebrity press, it doesn't make anyone the least bit happier.

So we decided to get a realistic hold on things. We thought: most of the time we don't have darkly cloaked, menacing figures lurking outside or crocodile-infested swamps to negotiate. Rarely is there even a remote possibility of a helicopter to jump out of. And there definitely (so far at least) never appeared on the 'to do' list a million-dollar decision to make about whose company or which Côte d'Azur villa to buy, or where to invest an enormous bonus courtesy of the chairman. Most of the time, we're mending a fuse in the dark, making mustard and cress sandwiches, removing a splinter from our kid's toe, fighting the slugs in the garden and chasing a spider out of aunt Hilda's lacy cardigan.

We thought a bit more about the reality of life and one day came up with a novel idea: it doesn't have to be dull. We compiled a list of tasks undergone on an average day and took a step back. So much activity, scale, variety – words not normally associated with such meagre undertakings. Then we realised. This slice of ordinary life staring back at us was beginning to look amusing, not average at all. The dreams of money, success and adventure were starting to blur.

That's how we came to put together this book. If you're ready for a slice of real life, but scared it will be tedious, try completing the annual programme of 52 tasks. Check your progress and perfect your skills as you go along using the performance assessments, and see how much better you feel. There's no final score to add up or golden prize to collect – remember, we're talking low ambition here – just individual tasks to do well in your own way. Simple as that.

Who needs a big mountain to climb when a little one will do?

WEEK 1

MAKING A BED WITH HOSPITAL CORNERS

★

Bed making is a skill that requires precision and dedication for a perfect result. Wear clean clothes, comfortable shoes and take off protruding jewellery before you start. Keep an upright position, with shoulders back and weight evenly balanced on both legs. When finished the bed should look immaculate, with tight, crisp edges and not a wrinkle in sight. The time allowed for completion is 10 minutes.

You will need: bed, bottom sheet, flat top sheet, blanket, pillow, pillowcase.

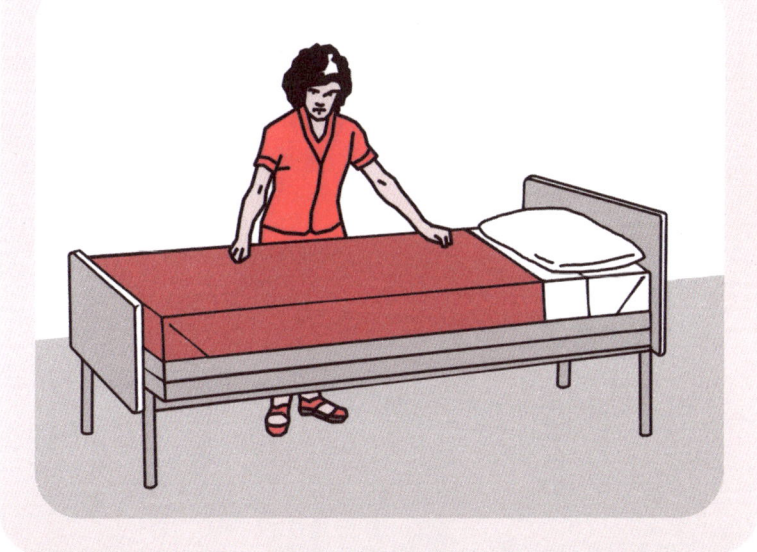

TECHNIQUE

1. Place the bottom sheet on the bed
Make sure the centre fold of the sheet is aligned to the centre of the mattress. Tuck in firmly under the mattress, starting at the foot of the bed.

2. Spread the top sheet
Put the large hem at the head of the bed. Make sure the sheet hangs evenly on both sides of the bed.

3. Add the blanket
Fold the blanket lengthwise and place it so the centre fold is centered on the bed *(a)*. The top should be 6 inches (15 cm) from the head of the mattress. Tuck in at the foot of the bed *(b)*. Fold the top sheet back 4 inches (10 cm) over the blanket.

a. Make sure the top sheet and blanket are centered on the mattress.

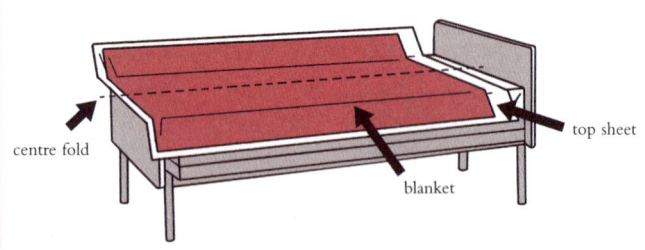

b. Tuck in tightly at the foot of the bed.

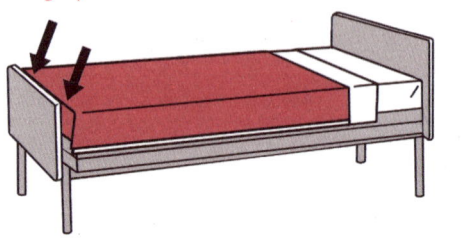

4. Make a hospital corner

Pick up the top sheet and blanket at one corner, approximately 12 inches (30 cm) from the foot of the bed, and fold them back to form a triangle on top of the mattress *(c)*. Tuck the hanging portion under the mattress. Bring the triangle back over the side of the mattress so it hangs down. Tuck in along the side of the bed *(d)*. Repeat on the other side.

5. Add the pillowcase

Hold the pillowcase at the centre of the seam, then turn the case back over your hand. Grasp the pillow through the case at the centre of one end. Bring the case down over the pillow. For best results place the pillow on the bed with the open end of the pillowcase facing away from the door.

c. Make a hospital corner by lifting up a corner and laying it across the bed.

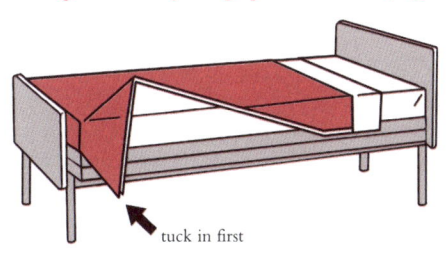

d. Tuck in along the side of the bed.

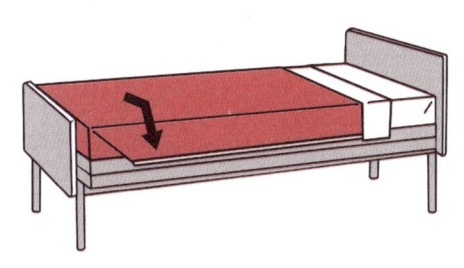

PERFORMANCE INDICATOR

★

A coin will bounce on a tightly-made bed (the US Army quarter-bounce test).

FOR HIGH FLYERS

★

Rotate the mattress four times a year, at each change of season. This is a good time to wash all bed linens.

★

Flip the mattress over twice a year.

WARNING

★

Don't confuse a hospital corner with an apple-pie bed. An apple-pie bed is made with a sheet folded so that the legs of the occupant cannot be stretched out.

IDENTIFY STRENGTHS AND AREAS FOR IMPROVEMENT

★

Tick the correct score bubble:

	bad	fair	good	very good	excellent
Dress and posture	0 1	2 3 4	5 6	7 8	9 10
Technique	0 1	2 3 4	5 6	7 8	9 10
Appearance of finished product	0 1	2 3 4	5 6	7 8	9 10
Comfort test	0 1	2 3 4	5 6	7 8	9 10

Total score —————— **Evaluator** ——————

Score: ★★★ 33–40 / ★★ 17–32.99 / ★ 5–16.99 / Try again 0–4.99

WEEK 2

DECIPHERING A UTILITY BILL

★

Deciphering a utility bill will test your powers of deduction, and your patience. Try to keep a calm, clear head when faced with perplexing charges, baffling fees, rate and tariff changes, formulas, consumption readings and billing calculations. The experience is especially rewarding if overcharges or unauthorized changes can be detected and resolved.

You will need: gas bill, electricity bill, telephone bill, calculator

TECHNIQUE

1. Check the terms of your Service Agreement
First check if you have a variable rate plan or a fixed rate plan for each of the utility services. If you have a bundled 'package', check the services you have signed up for (e.g. phone packages might include line rental, call waiting, voicemail, unlimited local calls and special long distance rates in return for a monthly fee).

2. Check the service charges
On each monthly utility bill, check that the service charges correspond to your Terms of Service Agreement. Service charges range from telephone line rental fees to a charge for the privilege of having a service.

3. Check if the rates or tariffs on the bills are correct
On each monthly utility bill, check that the prices per unit match the rates in your Terms of Service Agreement.

4. Check the charge for units used on your gas bill
Check that your gas meter reading corresponds to the bill reading. Subtract the reading last time from the reading now to find the units used in cubic metres. To this figure you may need to apply a multiplier to adjust to standard pressure conditions (the multiplier should be shown on the bill). To calculate the units used in terms of kilowatt hours (kWh), multiply the number of cubic metres of gas used by the calorific value (the energy content of the gas) and divide by 3.6. Multiply the number of kWh by the price per unit to find how much you owe.

5. Check the charge for units used on your electric bill
Check that the electric meter reading corresponds to the bill reading. Subtract the reading last time from the reading now to find the number of units used. Multiply this figure by the price per unit to find how much you owe.

6. Check the charge for calls made on your phone bill

Check that the itemised calls are correct, the price per call has been calculated at the right rate, and any calls included in a monthly pre-paid package have not been charged twice.

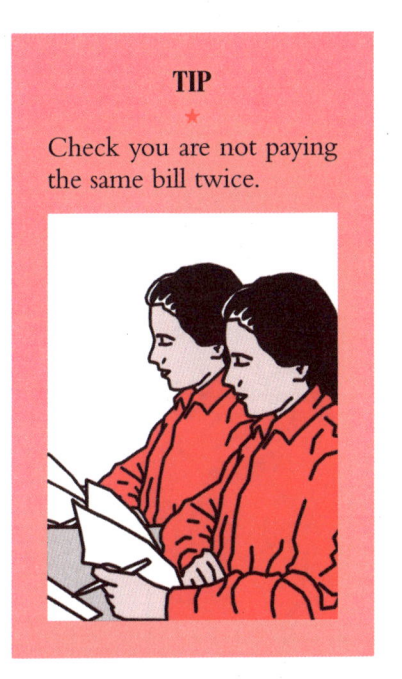

IF YOU ENJOYED THIS
★
Try a career in accountancy.

TIP
★
Check you are not paying the same bill twice.

PERFORMANCE ASSESSMENT
★
Ask the utility company for an honest assessment:

Try harder	Couldn't find any monthly bills	0 points
★	Fell asleep	1 point
★★	Couldn't find gas meter	2 points
★★	Couldn't find a calculator	2 points
★★★★	Found a discrepancy and received a rebate	100 points

WEEK 3

CHANGING A LIGHT BULB

★

There are plenty of potential hazards in changing a light bulb. Elevated structures used to climb and reach a light fitting may collapse suddenly. Stiletto heels, if worn, can cause accidents when mounting a ladder. Wet hair from a recent bath may result in an electrical shock. To complete this task safely, wear dry rubber gloves, boots, eye protection and a hat. Remember that electricity can kill. If in doubt, call an electrician.

You will need: portable ladder, scaffold, pole or similar elevated structure, proper clothing and safety equipment, torch, replacement bulb, assistant, handkerchief

TECHNIQUE

1. Be prepared
Keep a torch handy in case a bulb goes during night hours. Keep a notebook to record light fittings and bulb types in your home. Keep a stock of light bulbs, and a stock list.

2. Switch off
Switch off at the light switch. De-energise all electrical circuits by switching off at the mains.

3. Position the ladder
Position a portable ladder on even flooring below the pendant light fitting, approximately 6 inches (15 cm) to the left of a vertical trajectory from the pendant to the floor if you are right-handed, and an equal distance to the right if you are left-handed.

4. Prior to climbing
Engage ladder locks or braces. Check the ladder is high enough to reach the light fitting without stretching or assuming a hazardous position. Check for loose hinges, rungs or screws. Clean off any liquids or mud that have accumulated on the treads, and dry the ladder afterwards.

5. Safety equipment
If worried about safety, now is a good moment to put on eye protection goggles, safety belt, harness, drop line, lanyard, lifeline and rubber suit.

a. Bayonet cap bulb: push gently into light fitting and twist clockwise.

6. Mount the ladder and remove the bulb
Ask your assistant to hold the ladder. Stay in the centre while climbing, hold the side rails with both hands, and avoid going too high. Taking care not to lose your balance, unscrew the broken bulb, using a handkerchief if hot, and pass to assistant.

b. Screw cap bulb: screw clockwise into holder.

7. Replace the bulb
Take replacement bulb from assistant. Hold glass bulb firmly in one hand and light fitting in the other. Being careful not to touch metal parts, push metal end of bulb into holder. Twist gently clockwise for bayonet cap bulb, until bayonet pins slot into place. Screw into holder for screw cap type, until it sits firmly in the light socket.

8. Test the bulb
Get down from the ladder, turn on the mains supply and try the light switch.

ADVICE FOR LESS NIMBLE PEOPLE
★
Use low energy light bulbs, which need changing less often.

HAZARDS

★

Electrical shock. *Assistant:* Switch off the electricity at the mains. Wearing dry rubber gloves or with several layers of dry newspaper, drag the victim away from the electrical source. Call for medical help. Apply first aid for electrical injury, including Cardio Pulmonary Resuscitation if required. Don't touch burns, blisters or remove burned clothing.

★

A fall. *You:* Don't panic, assess the situation and determine if you are hurt. Regain your composure before getting up. If seriously injured, your assistant should call for medical help.

PERFORMANCE ASSESSMENT

★

Injuries serious	**0 points**
Injuries slight	**1 point**
No injuries	**2 points**
No injuries, light bulb changed	**10 points**

WEEK 4

GETTING THE RIGHT TONE ON AN ANSWERING MACHINE

*

Whether its a light-hearted message for friends or a serious, business-style recording, having the right thing to say and saying it well can help build your image and influence. Before recording an outgoing message, be clear about the effect you want. Practise different types of message and choose the one that feels natural.

You will need: telephone, answer machine

TECHNIQUE

1. A joke message
Unless you know a very good joke and can deliver it in an original way, don't bother *(a)*.

2. A message for avoiding people
An off-putting outgoing message can cut down the number of incoming messages by half. For example: 'Hello, I'm probably at home. I'm just avoiding someone I don't like. Leave me a message, and if I don't ring back, it's you.' If you prefer more subtle means, try making the outgoing message very, very long.

3. A sensible message: simple and to the point
Straightforward, short messages of the sort, 'Hello, we can't take your call right now, so please leave your message after the tone' are suitable for a range of callers from friends to time-share holiday sales representatives and business colleagues.

a. A joke must be good and delivered well.

4. Practise your message
When you have memorised your message, practise speaking it to make a vocal impact. Avoid mumbling the words in a monotonous tone. Develop clarity and a pleasant style: keep your throat relaxed while speaking, move your jaw properly to articulate the words, and project your speech with a strong outflow of air pushed out by the abdominal muscles. Do not force loudness from the voice box as this will sound strained. Speak in a natural pitch for your voice.

5. How to disguise your voice

You may not want your callers to recognise your voice. A simple way to disguise a voice is to whisper, though it may not record well. Another technique is to place a pencil between your teeth to affect tongue and jaw movement. This can fool even members of your own family.

6. Record your message

Finally, follow the instructions on your answer machine to record your chosen message. Avoid putting on an artificial recording voice, unless this is your intention.

b. Put a pencil between your teeth to disguise your voice.

FOR HIGH FLYERS

★

Practise outgoing messages from one of the following: • Sports coach • Member of the clergy • Lawyer • Teacher • Sales representative • Computer voice simulator

---

PERFORMANCE ASSESSMENT

★

Ask an incoming caller to give an honest assessment:

	bad	fair	good	very good	excellent
Message content	0 1	2 3 4	5 6	7 8	9 10
Message clarity	0 1	2 3 4	5 6	7 8	9 10
Vocal image	0 1	2 3 4	5 6	7 8	9 10
Naturalness/Disguise	0 1	2 3 4	5 6	7 8	9 10

Total score _____ **Evaluator** _____

Score: ★★★ 33–40 / ★★ 17–32.99 / ★ 5–16.99 / Try again 0–4.99

WEEK 5

MAKING TOAST

★

Owning a pop-up toaster is an important first step in any toast-cooking career, but you still need precision skills to achieve a perfect slice of toast. Acquire them by visiting known toast-making establishments and observing the transformation of limp slices of white bread to golden-brown crispy toast. Then practise at home following the advice outlined here.

You will need: pop-up toaster, slice of bread

TECHNIQUE

1. Select the bread
Wholegrain and rye breads make very good toast but for a thoroughly miraculous transformation buy the limpest, lightest textured sliced white bread you can find in the supermarket.

a. Turn the browning button to medium.

2. Place bread in toaster
Open bread packet and place selected pieces into toaster slots.

3. Start toasting
Turn the browning button to medium *(a)* and press down the starter button to begin toasting.

4. Assess the results
When the toast pops up, if it is not golden on both sides then repeat, turning the browning button up or down as necessary.

5. Progressing to grill
Using a grill is probably the only way to achieve perfect, evenly-browned toast, but it is also more challenging. Turn the grill on medium high and select the required number of slices, spacing them evenly on the grill pan. When the bread has turned to a crisp golden-brown, quickly flip the pieces over and grill on the other side. Note that grilling usually takes less time for the second side because the grill is hotter.

6. Use a toast rack
Always put toast in a toast rack to avoid sogginess.

WARNING

★

Do not fall asleep in a chair after putting your toast under the grill.

FOR HIGH FLYERS

★

Toast a bread bun on a long toasting fork over a camp fire.

PERFORMANCE ASSESSMENT
★

Ask someone who appreciates toast to give an honest assessment:

Try again	Limp, soggy, inedible	0 points
★	Burnt on both sides	1 point
★★	Burnt on one side	2 points
★★★	Crisp and golden-brown all over	100 points

WEEK 6

KEEPING A FISH IN A FISH BOWL

★

Despite what everyone thinks, goldfish are not the right fish for fish bowls. They grow too quickly and produce too much harmful waste, making the water turn cloudy in no time. Choose a smaller fish and put it in a big bowl. Practise your water-changing and bowl-cleaning skills and aim to keep the fish alive more than a few weeks.

You will need: big fish bowl (over 1 gallon capacity or 4.5 l), small fish, cultured gravel, water plants, small fish net, fish food, Lost City of Atlantis and other ornaments

TECHNIQUE

a. Fill the bowl with water, but not right to the top.

1. Add water to fish bowl
The fish bowl should be filled with at least a gallon (4.5 l) of water, of the correct pH and hardness for your chosen fish *(a)*. Use bottled water to be sure of no added chlorine. Check with your fish shop for any special requirements, including nutrients for your fish.

2. Add cultured gravel, water plants and ornaments
At the bottom of the bowl place a good covering of cultured gravel. This is available from fish shops and contains 'friendly' bacteria that digest fish waste, helping to keep the water clear. Add oxygenating plants, rocks, a Lost City of Atlantis and other decorations, but leave enough space for the fish.

3. Add the fish
Before setting the fish free, float the fish bag on top of the water for half an hour, until the temperature of the water in the bag is the same as the water in the bowl *(b)*. Then open the bag a little, allowing some of the bowl water and the bag water to mix. Close the bag and repeat every 15 minutes until the water is thoroughly mixed and the fish happily swims out into the bowl.

b. Float the bag on top of the water in the bowl.

4. Feed the fish

Use fish food bought from the fish shop and feed twice a day. Don't feed more than the fish will eat *(c)*. Any food that sinks to the bottom of the bowl will pollute the water and should be removed after the feed.

5. Change the water

If the water becomes cloudy or yellow, or if it is changed all in one go, the fish will suffer. No more than 10 to 20 per cent of the existing water should be changed at a time, and any new water must be the same pH, temperature and type as the old. Aim to change water twice a week.

6. Clean the bowl

Every few weeks pour off most of the water into a container, where the fish, once caught with a net, can be placed temporarily. Remove and clean the ornaments, scrub the algae on the inside of the bowl and discard the remaining soiled water. Return the fish and top up with clean water as in *(5)* above.

c. Do not feed more than the fish will eat.

TIPS

★

Don't buy a big fish for a small bowl.

★

A fine mesh cover over the top of the bowl will stop the fish from jumping out and the cat from sticking its paw in.

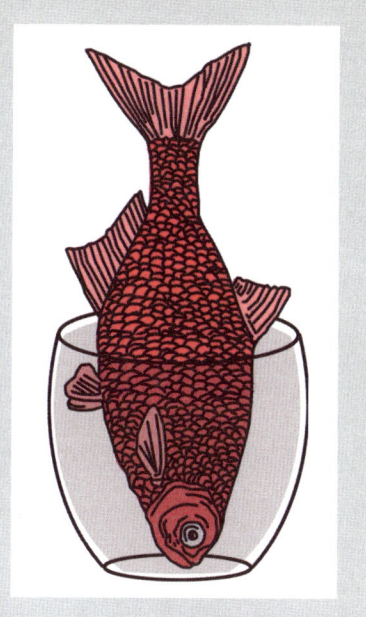

PERFORMANCE ASSESSMENT
★

Ask a fish consultant to give an honest assessment:

Try harder	Fish disappears	**0 points**
★	Fish dead after 1 week	**0.5 points**
★★	Fish dead after 3 weeks	**1 point**
★★★	Fish alive after 3 years	**100 points**

WEEK 7

GIVING A MASSAGE

★

The aim of this task is not to become a fully qualified therapeutic masseur (which could take years) but to give a relaxing back massage to your partner to remove tension and improve circulation. Go slowly and smoothly, responding to your partner's reactions, and remember that the objective is to loosen the muscle tissue, not the skin – or anything else.

You will need: willing partner, massage oil, firm mattress, towel, warm and quiet place

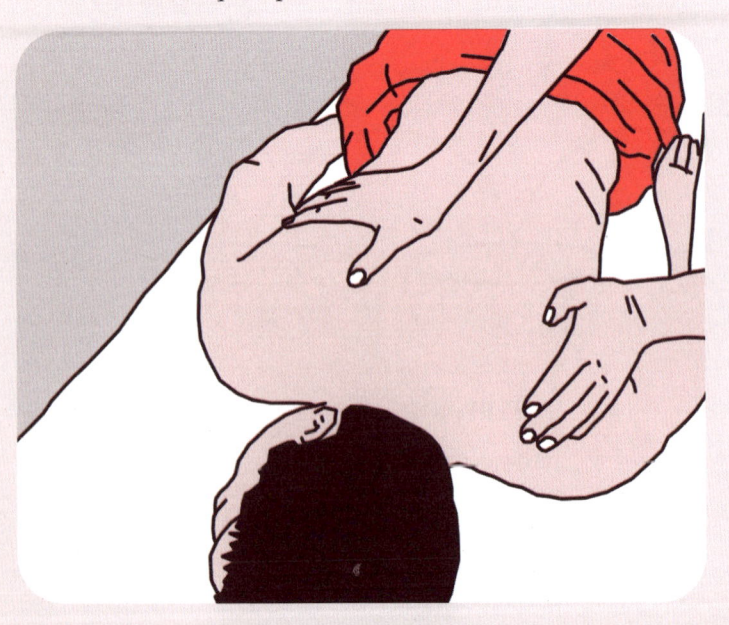

TECHNIQUE

1. Dress appropriately
Avoid wearing draping clothes, nail extensions, jewellery or strong perfume.

2. Prepare for the massage
Ask your partner to lie face down on a towel on a firm mattress, preferably naked, at least from the waist downwards. The room should be warm and quiet, the atmosphere relaxing (soft music, low light, a pleasant aroma may help).

3. Apply massage oil
Make sure your hands are not cold. Warm the massage oil by placing the bottle in a bowl of hot water and working the oil in your fingers. Apply the oil evenly over the neck, shoulder blades and back.

4. Apply relaxing strokes that improve circulation
With both hands placed flat on the lower part of the back, on either side of the spine, move them up the muscles running parallel with the spine, across the shoulder blades, and on the way back take in the shoulders and lower neck in one smoothly curving pattern *(a)*. Use light to medium pressure through your palms and fingers, keeping the strokes rhythmic and even. Do not touch the spine. Repeat 10–20 times.

a. With both hands flat, follow a smooth, curving pattern over the back.

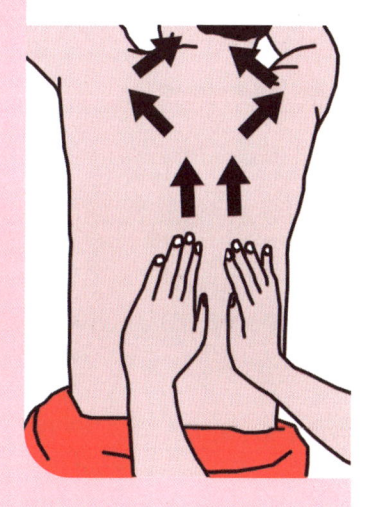

b. Knead the muscles between your fingers and thumbs.

5. Work deeper into the muscles

Once your partner is relaxed, apply a little more pressure, kneading the muscles between your fingers and thumbs. Focus on the ridge of muscles that run either side of the spine (again, do not touch the spine) and the muscles around the shoulder blades and at the base of the neck, spending more time on any that are tight with tension.

6. Finish with smooth circles and a lighter touch

Finally, run your fingers over the muscles in light, circular movements to fully relax your partner and signal the end of the massage.

WARNING

★

Be prepared to give regular massages if you are good at it.

PERFORMANCE ASSESSMENT

★

Ask your partner to give an honest assessment:

Partner requires physiotherapy afterwards	**0 points**
Partner screams throughout	**1 point**
Partner says it tickles and asks you to stop	**2 points**
Partner moans ecstatically throughout	**50 points**

WEEK 8

DETERRING
A BURGLAR

★

It pays to make it difficult to break into your home: most opportunist burglars give up if it takes more than five minutes to enter. The skill in deterring a burglar is to make enough visual and audible deterrents to ensure they don't even try to find a weak spot. Develop your deterrence strategy and you will reduce the chances of getting hit.

You will need: DIY skills or a locksmith and other specialists, good security routines, dog (optional)

TECHNIQUE

1. Fit strong locks
Install deadlocks on all external doors and keyed locks on all windows, including small ones. Make sure external doors and door frames are solid and strong. Lock up whenever you go out. Don't leave a spare key in an obvious place like under the mat.

2. Keep your home well lit
Fit security lighting with infra-red sensors around the exterior of the building. Leave interior lights on a timer when you go out *(a)*.

3. For vulnerable basement or ground floor windows
Fit security grills.

4. Consider installing a burglar alarm
Ideally, get an alarm that connects to a security firm. Or get a fierce-looking dog *(b)*.

a. Leave interior lights on a timer switch when you go out.

5. Keep valuables hidden from view
Make sure electrical and other valuable equipment is not visible from outside.

6. Create exterior barriers
Strong garden fencing, thorny bushes and crunchy gravel may help to deter a burglar, but keep hedges and fences low onto the street so neighbours can spot anything suspicious. Do not leave a ladder outside where a thief can use it *(c)*.

b. Get a dog that barks.

7. When you go away
Do not advertise your away dates on your answering machine or by discussing them in a public place. Arrange for a neighbour to check the house regularly, draw curtains and take in mail. Keep interior lights and a talk radio on timer switches.

c. Don't leave a ladder handy for a thief to use.

FOR HIGH FLYERS

★

Capture a burglar on video.

IDENTIFY STRENGTHS AND AREAS FOR IMPROVEMENT

★

Ask a policeman (or a thief) to give an honest assessment:

	bad	fair	good	very good	excellent
Locks	0 1	2 3 4	5 6	7 8	9 10
Alarms	0 1	2 3 4	5 6	7 8	9 10
Security routine	0 1	2 3 4	5 6	7 8	9 10
Extra gadgets	0 1	2 3 4	5 6	7 8	9 10

Total score _____ **Evaluator** _____

Score: ★★★ 33–40 / ★★ 17–32.99 / ★ 5–16.99 / Try harder 0–4.99

WEEK 9

DISGUISING A LACK OF KNOWLEDGE

★

Finding yourself amongst a group of people with superior knowledge can be embarrassing. The challenge in disguising your ignorance is not to resort to a whole lot of words that mean nothing. Far better to appear mysterious or to probe for information. If you feel you are in seriously deep water, steer the topic towards something you know more about, or feign a sudden illness.

You will need: knowledgeable friends, a party or pub where you can talk, embarrassing holes in your knowledge

TECHNIQUE

1. Let the conversation flow
Once seated in a comfortable place, the conversation will naturally find a range of topics, and your limitations will soon become apparent. But don't let anyone know this.

2. Avoid speaking loudly about nothing
Do not launch into the conversation if you can add nothing sensible or interesting. Do not try to disguise a dull point with fancy or technical language. Don't underestimate your friends: someone will see through you.

3. Learn to listen
Listen carefully to what is being said *(a)*. Try to identify holes in the logic to an argument or examples that are unclear. Listen and nod slowly if you think the speaker is on the right track. Furrow your brow and purse your lips in a discerning way if you discover a point that seems suspect.

a. Try to look interested while listening.

4. Test the speaker's knowledge
Even if your knowledge is weak you can test the speaker's by asking for details or gently questioning her logic or approach ('Couldn't this be seen differently?'). Alternatively, look for another way to express her thoughts, or ask for a different example if hers is unclear.

5. Think laterally

Though you may not know anything about the topic under debate, there will be parallels or links to subjects about which you do have knowledge. Move the topic subtly towards your goal. If you have something fascinating to say, you'll take the audience with you.

TIP

Disguising a lack of knowledge isn't necessary in some jobs.

PERFORMANCE ASSESSMENT

Interrupted speaker and talked monotonously for 10 minutes about something no one can remember	0 points
Made speaker look small after showing her argument to be paper thin	1 point
Said nothing and looked embarrassed	2 points
Made a mysterious interjection no one quite understood	5 points
Helped speaker to clarify her point and shifted subject to new topic, which most people found interesting	25 points

WEEK 10

BUILDING A SNOWDOME COLLECTION

★

Snowdome collecting is a secret passion for many people. If you cannot resist shaking a dome and watching the magical display of snow pieces gently drifting over a sentimental scene, then you have the potential to be a collector too. Before beginning, discuss the implications with family and close friends. Snowdomes are not designed to be hidden away in dark boxes. They require prominent display space and collectors have been known to redesign their homes for their domes.

You will need: display shelves, eye for tasteless objects, cash in varying amounts, restorer kits

TECHNIQUE

1. Finding snowdomes
Go to flea markets, airport gift shops or use the Internet to build your snowdome collection. Choose anything that takes your fancy. Older-style 'bas-relief' domes have tiny figures projecting from a painted background. Figurals are snowdomes in the shape of an object like a bear or a frog or a theme park. Mechanicals are snowdomes with a wind-up action. Calendar-based domes have a built-in revolving calendar in the base.

2. Refilling an empty snowdome
To refill an empty snowdome, remove the plug and fill with distilled water, using a clean eyedropper or a turkey baster *(a)*. Sealed domes are best left alone.

3. Dealing with marine life
Snowdomes stored away on dark shelves in holiday caravans tend to acquire undesirable marine life growing inside them.

a. Refill an empty snowdome using distilled water and a turkey baster.

Destroy it by adding a drop of bleach and placing the dome in a sunlit room (though not in direct sunlight).

4. Fixing scratches and scuff marks
Use a plastic polish kit to remove unsightly scratches on an old plastic dome *(b)*.

5. Making your own snow
Make your own snow by grinding up the mineral vermiculite. Alternatively, try introducing tiny, floating waterproof objects instead of snow, for example, inside a snowdome head you can have floating miniature brain parts.

6. Making your own snowdome
Buy a domes kit. You get a ready-made dome and base, a bag of snow, tube of glue, and tiny trees, sailboat, etc. Or create your own unique snowdome by introducing small, waterproof items of your choice.

b. Polish the dome to remove scratches.

WARNING

★

Displaying your snowdome in direct sunlight can cause fire.

★

Leaving a snowdome outside in freezing weather may cause it to crack.

★

Playing football with a snowdome is not recommended.

HOW TO JUDGE A GOOD COLLECTION

★

Origin	Bought in a Piccadilly Circus gift shop	Found in flea market	Hidden in grandmother's attic
Type	Plastic dome	Glass dome	Figural, plastic or glass
Size	Average	Unusually small	Unusually large
Contents	Buckingham Palace, silkscreen on flat panel	Fantastical scene: Peter Pan, flying trees and stardust	Wind-up theme park, giant 3-D moving statues, weird looking children in a big-dipper car
Score	★	★★	★★★

WEEK 11

REMOVING CAT HAIRS FROM A SUIT

★

Attending meetings, lunches or interviews with cat hairs on your suit can provoke raised eyebrows, even disgust when a hair attaches itself to papers or floats onto a colleague's crème caramel. Aim to deal with the problem at its source. Your success will depend on an integrated programme of prevention and removal.

You will need: cat, nice suit, cat brush, vacuum cleaner, washing machine, sticky-roller-tape hair remover

TECHNIQUE

1. Groom your cat
One of the best ways of reducing hair in the house is to regularly groom your cat. Use a brush or comb suitable for your cat's hair type. Long-haired cats should be groomed every day; short-haired cats once or twice a week. Groom the cat outside if you can.

2. Clean regularly
Vacuum the house regularly to remove hairs lying on the floor and furniture. Train the cat not to jump on chairs or on the bed. Make one place his bed and wash the cover regularly.

3. Store your suit carefully
Keep it in a closed cupboard or inside a plastic suit cover.

4. Feed the cat before you put on your suit
If you don't, your cat will wind itself around your suit legs while you open the tin, covering them with hair.

a. Use a sticky-roller-tape hair remover on your suit.

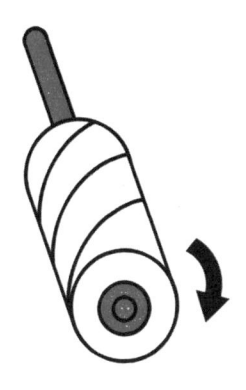

5. Put on your suit
Dress in a clean room, far away from the cat.

6. Use a pet-hair remover
Before leaving the house, remove hairs from your suit using a sticky-roller-tape hair remover (a). Ask someone to pass the roller across your back and other places you cannot reach. Before leaving your car, pass the sticky-roller-tape hair remover over the suit once more.

DON'T TRY THIS

★

Using the suction head of a vacuum cleaner to remove loose hairs from a cat is cruel.

IDENTIFY STRENGTHS AND AREAS FOR IMPROVEMENT

★

Ask a cat-allergic friend to give an honest assessment:

	bad	fair	good	very good	excellent
Cat grooming routine	0 1	2 3 4	5 6	7 8	9 10
House cleaning routine	0 1	2 3 4	5 6	7 8	9 10
Putting on suit routine	0 1	2 3 4	5 6	7 8	9 10
Hair-free suit test	0 1	2 3 4	5 6	7 8	9 10

Total score _____ **Evaluator** _____

Score: ★★★ 33–40 / ★★ 17–32.99 / ★ 5–16.99 / Try harder 0–4.99

WEEK 12

CLEANING A CHANDELIER

The principles of cleaning a chandelier are the same whether it has 50 or 50,000 crystal pieces. The purpose of this task is to practise the traditional and satisfying technique of dismantling and washing each piece of crystal one by one. Keep a diagram of how you dismantle the pieces so you can fit them together again. The newly cleaned chandelier should sparkle and glow.

You will need: ladder, chandelier covered in dust and grime, distilled water, rubbing alcohol, mild detergent, thick quilt, ostrich feather duster, kitchen towel, cotton gloves

TECHNIQUE

1. Make a master diagram
Never dismantle a chandelier without first recording the positions of all removable parts on a piece of paper *(a)*.

2. Other preliminaries
Place a washable, spongy quilt underneath the chandelier in case pieces drop off. Switch the chandelier off at the light switch and the mains and wait for the light bulbs to cool. Arrange an alternative lighting source.

3. Lower the chandelier to eye level
Chandeliers installed on a winch can be lowered to the appropriate level. Otherwise, use a ladder on stable flooring to reach the fitting.

4. Dust first
Taking care not to rock the chandelier, use an ostrich feather duster to remove the worst layers of dust, catching the particles with a vacuum cleaner as they rise *(b)*.

5. Dismantle removable crystal pieces
Remove up to 15 pendants at a time, noting their positions on your diagram. Dip each one

a. Draw a master diagram recording positions of crystals.

b. Use an ostrich feather duster to remove the first layer of dust.

c. Wash each crystal pendant separately in a special solution.

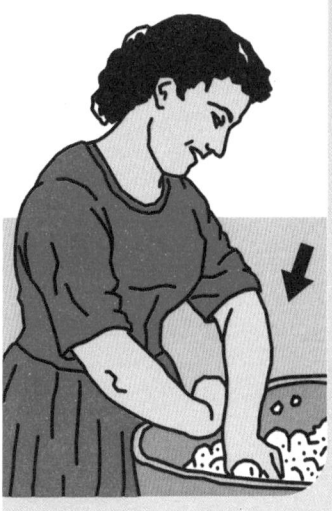

separately in a bucket filled with hot distilled water, two cups of rubbing alcohol and a small amount of mild detergent *(c)*. Wipe clean using a rag, and rinse.

6. Dry each piece, polish and return

Lay the pendants out on kitchen towel. Once dry, put on some cotton gloves and use a fresh kitchen towel to wipe away any remaining drops and give a final polish *(d)*. Return each crystal to its proper place. Don't forget to wipe clean the light bulbs and the main fixture before turning the power back on.

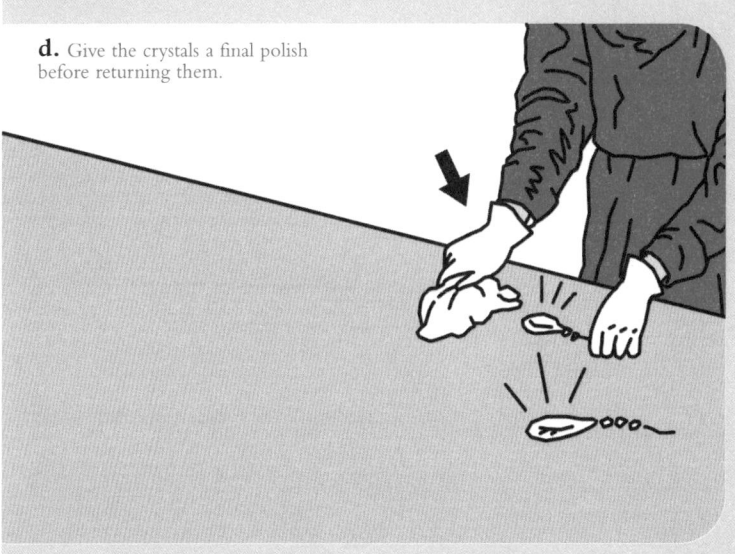

d. Give the crystals a final polish before returning them.

NOT RECOMMENDED

★

Washing your chandelier in a dishwasher.

★

Spraying your chandelier with a garden hose.

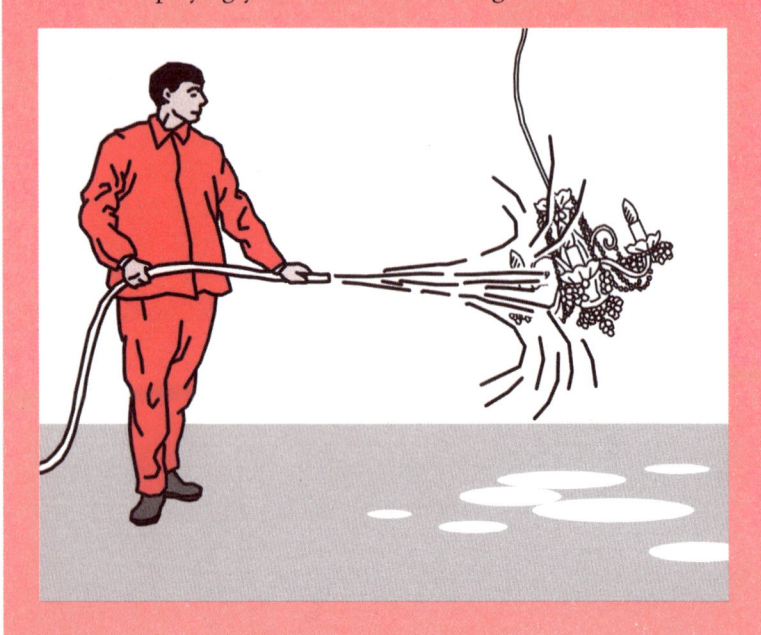

PERFORMANCE ASSESSMENT

★

Get someone to give an honest assessment:

Broken or chipped crystals	Completion time	Sparkle factor	Points
0–3	5 hours or more	★★★	30
4–8	3 hours or less	★★	10
9 or more	1.5 hours or less	★	5
whole fitting smashed	–	–	–30

WEEK 13

COPING WITH A HANGOVER

★

Sadly there is no miracle cure for the nausea, headache, dry mouth and general exhaustion that comes after drinking too much. But there are techniques to make the next 24 hours bearable, without resorting to more mind-altering substances (legal or illegal). The most difficult part of this task will be convincing yourself that another drink is not the only solution.

You will need: a night of alcohol excess, plenty of water, somewhere to sleep quietly, hospital visit (optional)

TECHNIQUE

a. Rehydrate by drinking plenty of water.

b. Try and eat something to replace your energy.

1. Drink lots of water
This will counteract the dehydrating effects of the alcohol *(a)*.

2. Eat something
Preferably not too heavy and it should include some protein *(b)*. A cooked breakfast if you can keep it down may help, but avoid large portions and too much grease. If you feel nauseous, try nibbling dry crackers or biscuits.

3. Go for a walk
A gentle walk in the fresh air will help to clear your head, but you will probably feel too exhausted to go far.

4. Have a rest
Find a cool, dark and quiet room to sleep. Your body needs time to recover.

5. Avoid more alcohol
It may lessen the immediate pain but it will prolong the period of hangover.

6. Avoid complicated tasks or conversations
Your concentration will not be at its best.

FOR HIGH FLYERS

★

Try coping with a hangover after several glasses of homemade elderflower wine.

AVOID

★

Practising this task too often.

EXTREME CASES

45

★

Go to hospital immediately.

PERFORMANCE ASSESSMENT

★

Ask yourself for an honest assessment:

Couldn't resist another drink	0 points
Sick constantly for 48 hours	0 points
Got fired	0 points
Went for a walk, slept and woke up feeling wonderful	25 points

WEEK 14

PLUGGING IN A VIDEO

★

The ability to plug in and set up a video or VCR is a skill still lacking in a high proportion of the population. The aim of this task is to connect a video cassette recorder to a TV and the power circuit, preferably without assistance, before the VCR becomes an obsolete piece of technology. It does not cover setting the time and date, recording, taping and playback, programming, tracking or Video Plus.

You will need: VCR, TV, aerial, cables, instruction manual

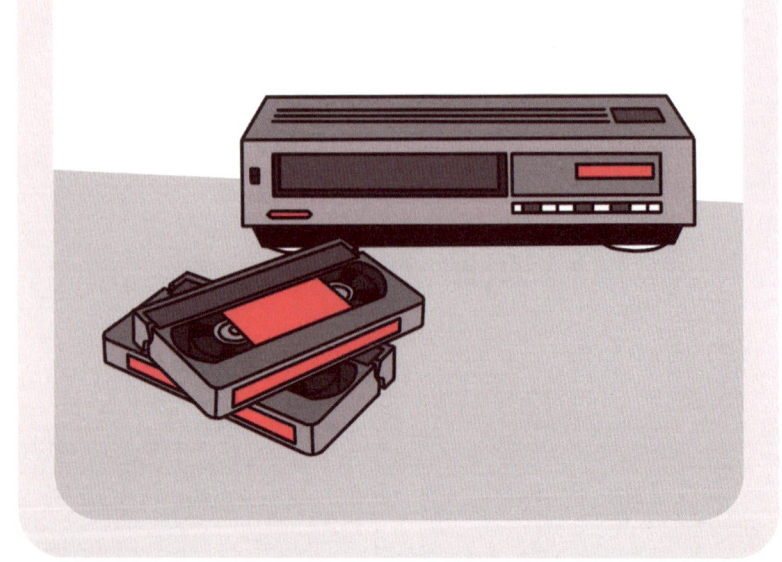

TECHNIQUE

1. Read the operating instructions
Before attempting to use the equipment, read the manufacturer's instructions, in particular the guidance for safe use.

2. Unplug from the mains
Make sure the VCR and TV are not connected to the mains supply.

3. Connect the aerial to the VCR
Connect the cable from your TV aerial (a coaxial cable made of two concentric conductors separated by insulating wire) to the RF IN terminal (*a in the diagram below*) of the VCR – this is the aerial terminal of the VCR, which receives the radio frequencies for TV stations.

4. Connect the aerial terminals of the VCR and TV
With a second coaxial cable, connect the RF OUT terminal (*b*) of the VCR to the aerial terminal (*c*) of the TV.

5. Connect the AV connector between the VCR and TV
With a EURO AV connector (a standard 21 pin connector supplied with your VCR) plug in one end to the VCR's EURO AV 1 IN/OUT socket (*d*) and the other end into the TV's EURO AV socket (*e*).

6. Switch on the mains supply
You can now plug in the VCR and TV.

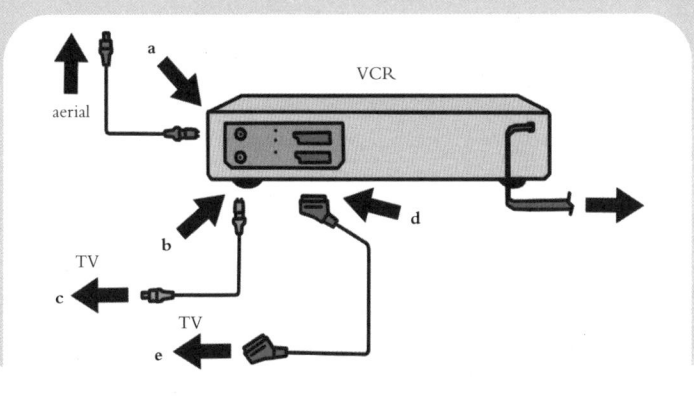

FOR HIGH FLYERS

★

Install batteries in the remote control:

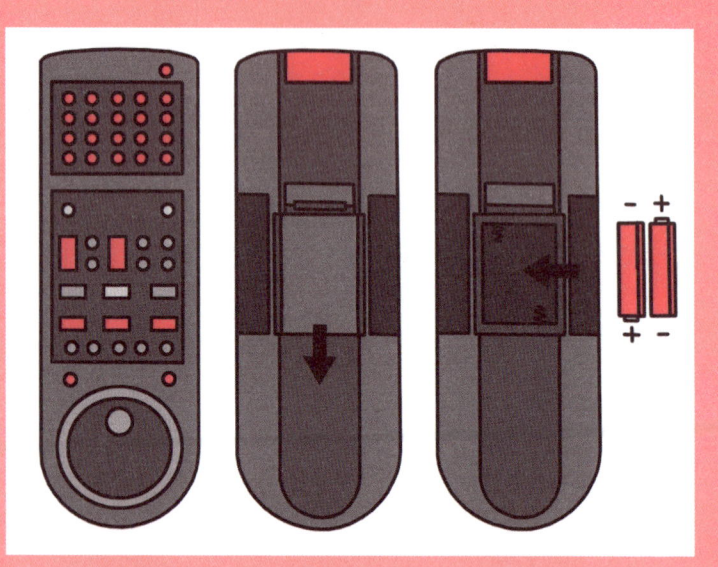

1. Unclip the cover to the battery compartment. **2.** Position the batteries ensuring that the polarity + and − of the batteries matches the polarity indicators inside the battery compartment. **3.** Replace the battery cover.

IDENTIFY STRENGTHS AND AREAS FOR IMPROVEMENT

★

Ask a technically-minded person to give an honest assessment:

	bad	fair	good	very good	excellent
Aerial connection	0 1	2 3 4	5 6	7 8	9 10
AV connection	0 1	2 3 4	5 6	7 8	9 10
Power connection	0 1	2 3 4	5 6	7 8	9 10
Safe practice	0 1	2 3 4	5 6	7 8	9 10
Total score		**Evaluator**			

Score: ★★★ 33–40 / ★★ 17–32.99 / ★ 5–16.99 / Get help 0–4.99

WEEK 15

MENDING A FLAT BICYCLE TYRE

★

Mending holes in inner tubes is a necessary part of cycling life. To complete the task comfortably and safely, carry with you a spare inner tube so you can mend the punctured tube when you get home – instead of beside a dual carriageway.

You will need: bicycle repair kit (rubber patches, glue, sandpaper), 2 tyre levers, pump, chalk or felt tip pen, spare inner tube (optional)

TECHNIQUE

1. Remove the wheel
Turn the bicycle upside down on flat ground, a safe distance away from any traffic. Remove the wheel using the quick release lever, or a dumbell if the fittings are conventional nuts and bolts.

2. Release one side of the tyre from the wheel
Let the air out of the tyre and pinch the tyre beads (inside edges) together to loosen them from the rim of the wheel. Insert a tyre lever underneath the tyre bead closest to you, somewhere away from the valve, and prise the bead over the wheel rim *(a)*. Use your thumbs to gently prise away the rest of the bead around the full circumference of the tyre.

a. Use a tyre lever to prise the tyre bead over the wheel rim.

3. Find the hole in the inner tube
Carefully pull out the inner tube. Pump it up and listen for the hiss of air from the hole, or submerge the tube in water and look for air bubbles *(b)*. Use chalk or a felt tip pen to mark a large cross over the hole.

4. Patch the hole
Sand the area around the hole, making the sanded area larger than the patch you are about to apply *(c)*. Spread a thin coat of glue

b. Submerge the tube in water and look for air bubbles.

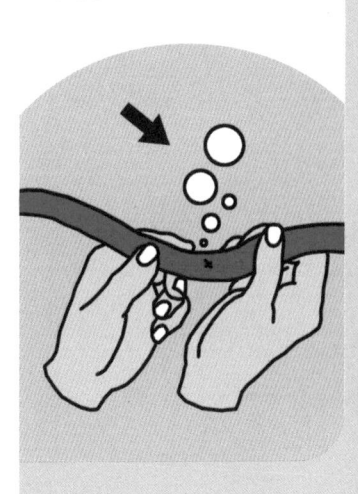

c. Sand the area around the puncture so the patch will stick.

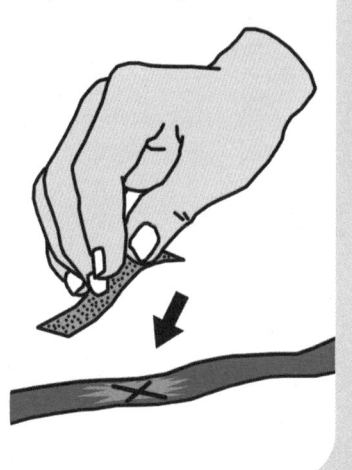

over the hole and on one side of the patch. Allow to dry for a minute before sticking the patch over the hole. Wait two minutes before peeling off the backing paper from the patch. Check the patch is glued all the way round.

5. Check the tyre
Before replacing the inner tube, check both the inside and outside of the tyre for thorns or other causes of the puncture. If you find a thorn, remove it by pulling from the outside of the tyre.

6. Replace the inner tube and wheel
When fully dry, put the repaired tube back inside the tyre, fitting the valve through the valve opening. Push the tyre bead back over the wheel rim, using both levers to ease the final section of bead into place. Replace the wheel and pump up the tyre.

TIPS FOR LESS PUNCTURES

★

Keep tyres properly inflated.

★

Ride slowly on rough surfaces.

WARNING

★

Bicycle repair patches are difficult to remove once glued.

PERFORMANCE ASSESSMENT

★

Ask a cyclist to give an honest assessment:

Lost the bicycle repair kit	**0 points**
Couldn't get the wheel off	**0 points**
Repaired tube went down within 5 minutes	**2 points**
Repaired tube still working	**10 points**

WEEK 16

MAKING A SPACE ROCKET MOBILE

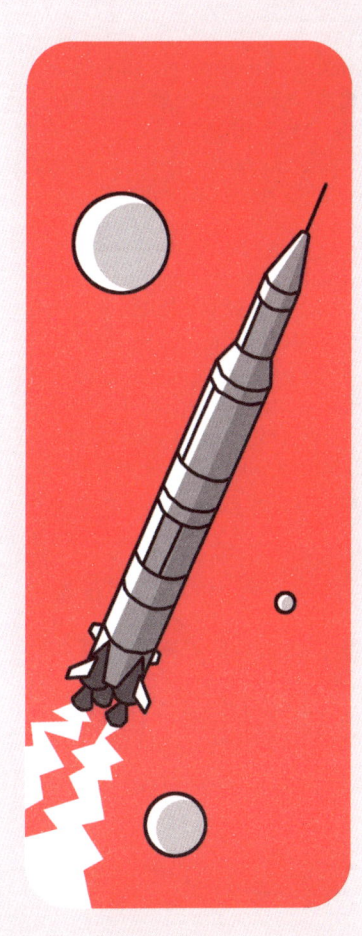

The Saturn-V space rocket, used for Nasa's 1969 and early 1970s Apollo Moon landings, and for launching the Skylab Space Station is probably the most famous of all space rockets, but a space rocket mobile of quality should also include a Russian Soyuz rocket with crew, several space stations, an alien space craft, planets of the inner and outer Solar System, and asteroids. Time allowed: 3 days.

You will need: large cardboard box, paper plates, scissors, cardboard cylinder tubes (from a kitchen roll or several toilet rolls stuck together), silver foil, polystyrene balls, ping pong balls, cotton wool, glitter in a range of colours, glue, paint brush, paints, strong button thread, large needle, metal eye-hook

TECHNIQUE

1. Make the mobile frame
Cut out two large circles of cardboard 20 inches (50 cm) in diameter *(a)*. Paint one side of each disc in black and stick the two discs together with the black facing outwards. Decorate with a spray of glitter on each side.

2. Attach strings for hanging the mobile to the ceiling
Cut three pieces of extra strong button thread, each approximately 2 feet (60 cm) long. Tie a large knot at the end of each piece. Using the needle, thread the three strings through the cardboard base at three equally spaced points around the disc *(b)*. Attach the loose ends to the metal eye-hook.

3. Make the Saturn-V and Soyuz rockets
Make a cone out of stiff paper, attach it to the end of a large cardboard kitchen roll tube, and cover the whole thing with silver foil *(c)*. Use black paint to indicate the three different stages of the rocket, and stick on Apollo mission logos. Cut out five small cones from the stiff card and attach to the base of the rocket to represent the engines, and from each engine glue strands of cotton wool to indicate smoke. Repeat for the Soyuz rocket, adapting to the Russian design as appropriate.

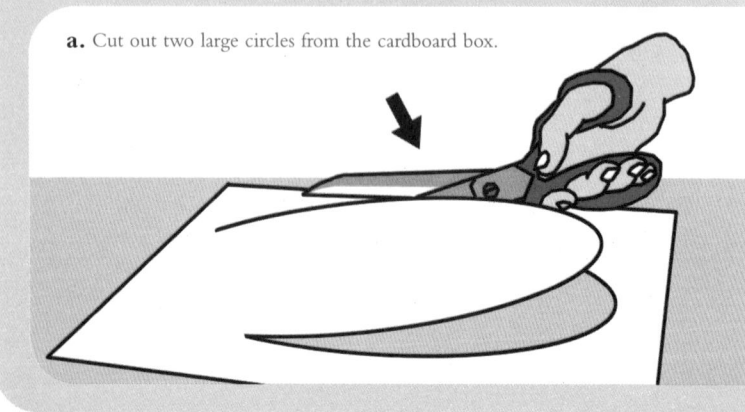

a. Cut out two large circles from the cardboard box.

b. Thread the strings through the base at equally spaced points.

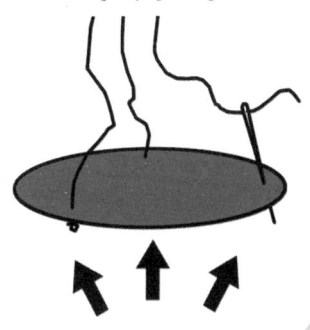

c. Attach cones to a kitchen roll tube to make a Saturn-V rocket.

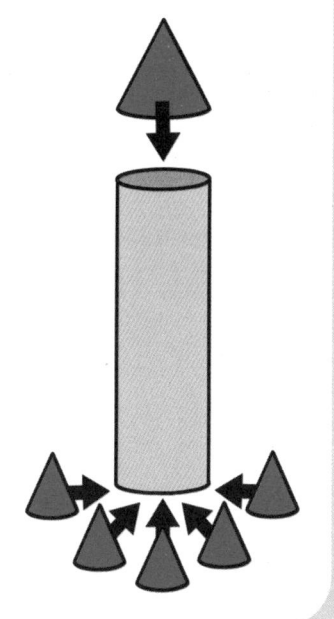

4. Make an alien space craft
Stick together two paper plates with the bases facing outwards. Cover in silver foil. Add some cut-out windows and draw in the alien pilots. Use glue to apply psychedelic glitter patterns on the exterior of the craft.

5. Make a solar system
Use polystyrene balls, ping pong balls and discs of stiff card to make a range of planets, including Neptune, Saturn, Jupiter, Earth, Pluto and Mars, painting and decorating each one in different colours. Cut a very large polystyrene ball in half, stick one half to the underside of the mobile disc, in the centre, and paint it yellow-orange to represent the sun.

6. Attach the spacecraft and planets to the mobile disc
Thread a piece of button thread with a large knot in the end through the top point of each craft or planet and the other end through the mobile disc, securing it with a discreet knot. Make sure the hanging pieces are well spaced and at different heights so they can spin unencumbered. Attach the mobile disc to the ceiling using the metal eye-hook.

HOT TIP

★

Be the first to hold a space rocket mobile party.

IDENTIFY STRENGTHS AND AREAS FOR IMPROVEMENT

★

Ask Mr Spock to give an honest assessment:

	bad	fair	good	very good	excellent
Space rockets	0 1	2 3 4	5 6	7 8	9 10
Aliens	0 1	2 3 4	5 6	7 8	9 10
Planets	0 1	2 3 4	5 6	7 8	9 10
Asteroids	0 1	2 3 4	5 6	7 8	9 10

Total score ──── **Evaluator** ────

Score: ★★★ 33–40 / ★★ 17–32.99 / ★ 5–16.99 / Try again 0–4.99

WEEK 17

REMOVING A SLUG OR SNAIL INFESTATION

★

A silver trail over a dahlia is sufficient evidence to begin a war against slugs and snails. To succeed in eradicating them, or at least controlling them – without resorting to chemical warfare – you will need planning skills, ingenuity and, if things get bad, a capacity for nastiness.

You will need: slug and snail infestation, beer, egg shells, copper tape, experimental approach

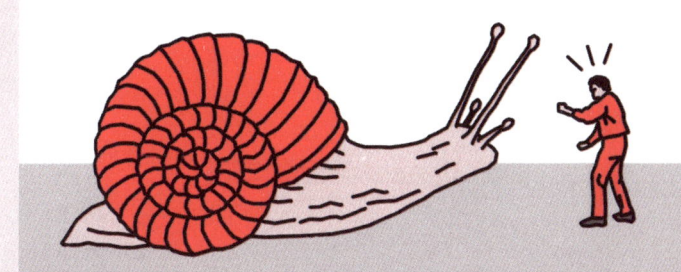

TECHNIQUE

1. Forcible removable
Pick up the slugs and snails, put them in a box and take them somewhere a long way away, for example, to another country. To find them during the day look under pieces of wood, pottery, plants, stones, damp logs, refuse, mulch and decaying leaves. The best time to catch them is in the late evening when they come out to feast *(a)*.

2. Trap them with beer
Alternatively, try baiting them with their favourite beverage. Pour beer into a shallow pan, where they will crawl, become intoxicated and drown *(b)*.

a. Find the snails and remove them.

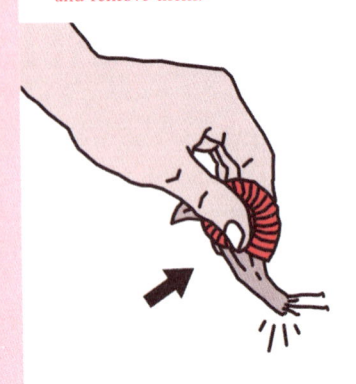

b. Drown the snails in beer.

c. Stop the snails with a ring of sharp shell pieces.

d. Shock the snails with copper tape.

3. Turn them away with egg shell circles

If you like eating eggs, another approach is to protect your favourite plants with a ring of broken egg shells around the base of each plant *(c)*. Slugs and snails dislike the sharp edges of the shells, and will move away rather than try to cross them. Remember that if the ring is broken they will quickly find a way through.

4. Shock them with copper tape

Copper tape around your plant pots or garden beds is another barrier worth trying *(d)*. The small electrostatic charge created when a slug or snail tries to pass over the copper tape is most unpleasant to them and will cause them to move away. You can buy copper tape at most garden centres.

5. Keep track of them

If you remove snails to another place, mark the top of their shells with nail varnish so you can check they are not finding their way 'home' again.

PRE-EMPTIVE ATTACK

★

Add salt and watch the slug dissolve.

WARNING

★

Slug colonies multiply when you go away on a long holiday.

WAR REPORT

★

Number of slugs & snails caught per day	Points to slugs & snails	Points to you
1	10	0
5	draw	draw
10	0	10

WEEK 18

KEEPING SOCKS IN PAIRS

There is an unwritten law that a sock drawer will always contain odd socks. It is both futile and tiresome to fight against it. However, there are strategies to lessen its impact. Successful completion of this task requires a strong commitment to the cause of keeping socks in pairs.

You will need: socks, washing machine, sock drawer, safety pins, ties, needle and thread, sock sorters (optional)

TECHNIQUE

a. Attach pairs of socks together as soon as you take them off.

1. Start afresh with new socks
Give away all your old socks or find alternative uses for them.

2. Buy new socks
Buy a large stock of new socks in just two colours of the same design. Choose contrasting colours (e.g. black and white) so you can sort your socks in the dark. Keep a few pairs in reserve to use for matching up with odd socks found later.

3. Organise your sock drawer
Insert a divider in your sock drawer to keep the two colours separate.

4. Washing and drying socks
This is when socks go missing. After washing and drying never throw all the socks into the drawer in one big heap. Organise them first, securing pairs together by turning over the tops. Any socks without a pair (there will always be at least one) should be placed in a separate box and matched to other single socks after each wash.

5. If problems persist
Attach pairs together as soon as you take them off – before they go into the laundry *(a)*. Do this by sewing tabs onto each sock and tying them together, by sticking them in pairs with velcro or a safety pin, or by buying washable sock sorters (plastic clips), which come in various colours and have the added advantage of distinguishing your sock pairs from other people's.

ALTERNATIVE TECHNIQUES

★

Dispense with the need for socks altogether by wearing longer trousers. Fold the extra length underneath the foot inside the shoe.

★

Permanently attach each sock to one end of a long piece of thin elastic.

USES FOR ODD SOCKS

★

• Stuff with dried peas and sew up the end to make a back massager. • Stitch the sock ends together and use as a sweat band.

PERFORMANCE ASSESSMENT

★

No. of odd socks:	after 1 week	after 2 weeks	after 3 weeks	after 4 weeks
1 point	5	10	15	20
5 points	4	8	12	15
10 points	2	4	8	10
20 points	1	2	3	4

Monthly score —————— Odd-sock recycling (bonus point) ——————

WEEK 19

MOWING A LAWN

*

Successful lawn management requires a responsible mowing regime. Cut the grass only when it is dry, keep your mower blades sharp, and cut frequently to a height suitable for grass type and growing season. Mowing regularly means grass clippings are short and can be left on the lawn to decompose.

You will need: mower, lawn, boiler suit

TECHNIQUE

1. Mowing frequency
When the grass is growing fastest, usually during the summer months, the lawn should be cut at least once a week, even twice a week. Mow less frequently in the autumn as growth rates decrease.

2. How much to cut
Follow the one-third rule: adjust the mower blades so they remove no more than one-third of the height of the grass at each mowing. In the spring, when the grass is long, adjust the blades to the highest setting.

3. Avoid a striped effect
Change the direction of mowing regularly to stop your lawn looking like a zebra.

4. In dry weather
Water the lawn and wait until it is dry before mowing *(a)*. Reduce the frequency of mowing and raise the blades a little.

a. Water the lawn in dry weather.

WARNING

★

Always keep your mower under control.

TIP

★

Do not adjust the mower blades while the motor is running.

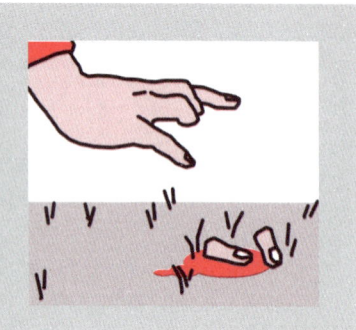

PERFORMANCE ASSESSMENT

★

★	A dense jungle of weeds	**try a scythe**
★★	Thin, stressed, yellow grass with brown patches, weeds, uneven height	**cut less grass more frequently**
★★★	Healthy green grass, dense coverage, even height	**good cutting**

WEEK 20

CHOOSING A TIE

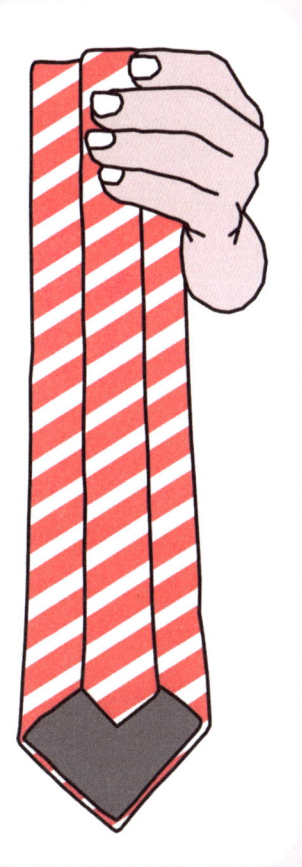

★

You need a critical eye to succeed at this task. Choosing the right tie involves finding one to match your figure, your personality, the clothes you are wearing and the occasion. There are numerous shapes, sizes, textures and qualitites of tie available, and as many potential pitfalls for you, the buyer.

You will need: range of ties, long mirror, tie-wearing occasion

TECHNIQUE

1. Choose an appropriate length and width of tie
Unless you want a 1970s look, keep to a standard width of between 3¼ and 3½ inches (8.25-9 cm). Most ties come in lengths of between 54 and 58 inches (137-47 cm). If you are tall, you may require a longer tie than this (after being tied, the two ends should nearly reach your waistband).

2. Select a tie pattern and colour to complement your clothes
If your suit is striped, choose a solid or patterned tie, or a tie with much thicker or thinner stripes than the suit stripes. If your shirt is loud with bright colours, choose a plain tie that doesn't compete. If your shirt is patterned (e.g. checked) and you want a patterned tie, make sure the patterns on the tie are much larger or smaller than the patterns on the shirt.

3. Select a tie pattern and colour to suit your looks
If you are short, try a dark-coloured tie with a strong vertical stripe. If you are tall and thin, you can wear a broader tie and brighter colours. If your complexion and hair colour strongly contrast (e.g. pale skin and dark hair), a strongly contrasting tie and suit/shirt should work well. If your complexion and hair colour do not contrast very strongly, try a tie and suit/shirt in grades of the same colour, rather than different colours.

a. A solid coloured tie works with a striped suit.

4. Choose a tie to match your personality, mood and the occasion

If you feel uncomfortable wearing a flamboyant tie then it's unlikely you'll carry it off. It will only make you embarrassed and unduly aware of the big thing around your neck. The occasion will usually dictate how formal or informal you need to be. Depending on your personality, you may occasionally break the rules and get away with it.

5. Stick to good quality

A good tie is generally made of smooth silk, has a 100 per cent wool lining and hangs straight without twisting.

b. A striped tie works with a solid coloured suit.

c. Mixing patterns and stripes can work if the contrast is great enough.

FOR HIGH FLYERS

★

Knotting a tie

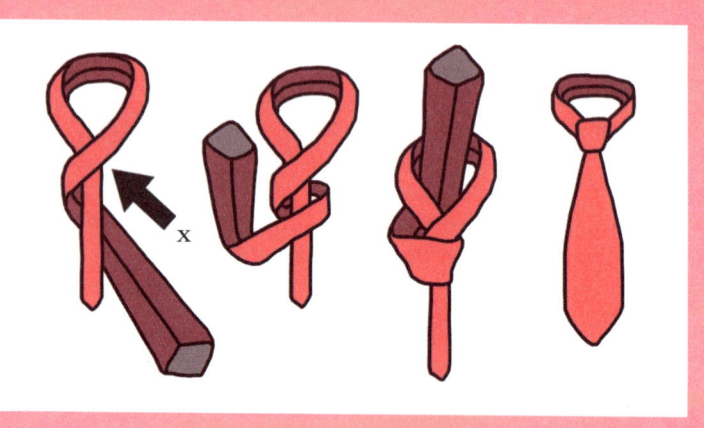

1. Hang the tie loosely around your neck. **2.** With your right hand, hold the narrow end at spot 'X', and with your left hand bring the broad end across the front of 'X' and hold it there with your right hand. **3.** With your left hand take the broad end behind and across in front of 'X' again. **4.** Then take the broad end behind 'X' and up through the 'V' at your neck. **5.** Allow the broad end to fall down through 'V', and tuck it between the top wrap of the knot formed at 'X'. **6.** Pull the broad end down and straighten the knot. **7.** The two ends should be the same length, or the broad end slightly longer than the narrow end. *[for right-handers, read 'right hand' instead of 'left hand']*

IDENTIFY STRENGTHS AND AREAS FOR IMPROVEMENT

★

Ask your butler to give an honest assessment:

	bad	fair	good	very good	excellent
Match of tie to suit	0 1	2 3 4	5 6	7 8	9 10
Match of tie to shirt	0 1	2 3 4	5 6	7 8	9 10
Match of tie to function	0 1	2 3 4	5 6	7 8	9 10
Tastefulness test	0 1	2 3 4	5 6	7 8	9 10

Total score ──────── **Evaluator** ────────

Score: ★★★ 33–40 / ★★ 17–32.99 / ★ 5–16.99 / Try harder 0–4.99

WEEK 21

REMOVING A SPIDER

★

If you suffer from arachnophobia you may be worried about this task. It's worth remembering that most spiders are harmless to humans and do a useful job of eating indesirable insects. The ones that bite do so only when handled or squashed. The Black Widow, for example, is one to avoid. Choose a common house spider instead.

You will need: common house spider, glass, a piece of stiff card, gloves, long-sleeved shirt

TECHNIQUE

1. Spying the spider
Do not jump up and down or run shrieking from the room. The spider will sense your unease and hide. Instead, quietly fetch a glass and stiff piece of card and approach the animal on tip toe. Wear gloves and a long-sleeved shirt if you are worried about the spider running up your arm.

a. Trap the spider inside a glass.

2. Place the glass over the spider
Avoiding sudden movements, lower the glass over the spider, trapping it inside without crushing its legs. Slide the card underneath the glass, carefully so the spider isn't harmed.

3. Dispose of the spider
Take the spider outside, as far away as possible from your house. Do not throw it out of the jar as this could seriously damage it. Instead, place the glass on its side on the grass and allow the spider to crawl out.

4. Spider on the ceiling
If you find a spider on the ceiling, do not bash it with a broom. Erect a ladder nearby and get as close as possible to the spider. Put the glass over the spider and slide the card between the glass and the ceiling *(a)*. Ask someone to hold the ladder while you do this.

WARNING

★

Do not use a duster to pick up a spider. A spider will escape from a duster and may run up your arm.

SPIDER-REMOVING TOOL

★

If a safe distance is preferred, create a spider-removing tool with a plastic cup fixed to a broom handle. Use a deep cup so the spider takes longer to crawl out. Meanwhile, get a friend to slip a piece of card across the top.

DON'T CONFUSE WITH

★

Spider veins. These are small blood vessels on the face and legs, which dilate with age and look like red spider webs.

PERFORMANCE ASSESSMENT

★

Ask someone brave to give an honest assessment:

★	Spider drops onto your head	**1 point**
★	Spider escapes and runs up your arm	**1 point**
★	Spider disappears into bed clothes	**1 point**
★★★	Spider is removed	**50 points**

WEEK 22

UNPLUGGING A CLOGGED SINK

A blocked or slow emptying sink caused by a build up of food, grease and other debris is a problem plaguing many households around the world. Most blockages can be unplugged without calling a plumber if you follow a few basic rules. It is better if you have some knowledge of how a sink works.

You will need: plunger, baking soda, hot water, piece of wire, adjustable wrench

TECHNIQUE

1. Check the grille of the waste outlet
First check to see if the grille across the waste outlet is clogged up. Pull out any trapped debris.

2. Remove blocked grease
If you suspect the problem is grease, pour four tablespoons of baking soda mixed with boiling water down the drain. The grease should dissolve and flow away when you follow this with a kettleful of boiling water.

3. Use a plunger
If the clog is still there, block up the sink overflow *(see a)* with a wet rag (and block the second drain if you have a double bowl sink). This stops pressure escaping when you apply the plunger.

a. Work out where the various parts of the sink are.

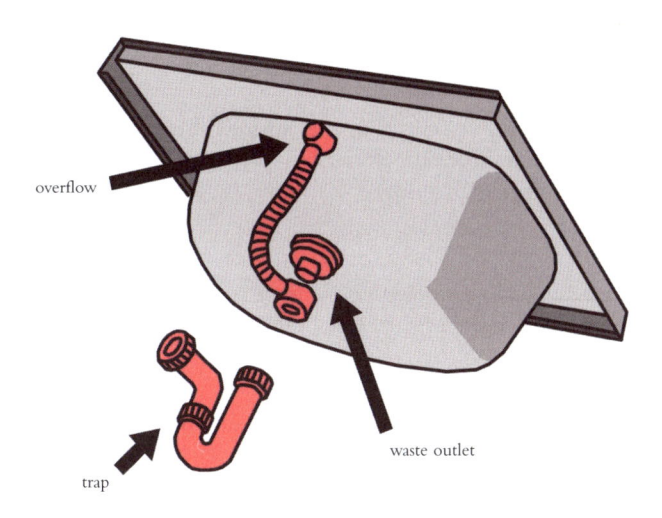

overflow

trap

waste outlet

Fill the sink with about 3 inches (8 cm) of hot water. Place the rubber plunger cup over the plug hole and pump up and down on the handle around 20 times. The pressure build up should push the clog through. Follow it with plenty of hot soapy water.

b. Unscrew the plastic coupling giving access to the trap.

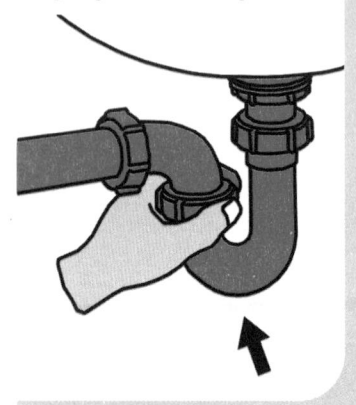

4. Clean the trap
If the previous steps haven't removed the blockage, locate the trap (the U-shaped fitting) under the sink and place a bucket under it. Unscrew the plastic coupling giving access to the trap and allow water from the trap to empty into the bucket *(b)*. Use a piece of wire to poke away any debris. Replace the fitting. A metal trap may have a cleanout plug at the bottom, which can be unscrewed using an adjustable wrench.

5. For blockages further down
If the clog isn't in the trap, and all above methods have failed, then the blockage is further down the pipe and it's probably time to call a plumber.

OTHER USES FOR PLUNGERS
★
- spider pick-up • large dart
- head massager

WARNING

★

Don't overdo it on the plunger.

IDENTIFY STRENGTHS AND AREAS FOR IMPROVEMENT

★

Ask a plumber to give an honest assessment:

	bad	fair	good	very good	excellent
Plunging technique	0 1	2 3 4	5 6	7 8	9 10
Trap-cleaning technique	0 1	2 3 4	5 6	7 8	9 10
Other uses for plunger	0 1	2 3 4	5 6	7 8	9 10

Total score ———— **Evaluator** ————

Score: ★★★ 33–40 / ★★ 17–32.99 / ★ 5–16.99 / Try again 0–4.99

WEEK 23

LIGHTING A BARBECUE

★

Most humans enjoy the taste of charcoal-grilled food but only a small proportion have mastered the skills of lighting a barbecue. To succeed you need perseverance, good equipment, a long fork and a cap to keep your hair tidy. Aim to have the coals turning to grey ash with a red-hot glow within 50 minutes of starting, ready for cooking to begin.

You will need: barbecue, charcoal, firelighters or newspaper, matches, prodding fork, tongs, proper barbecue dress

TECHNIQUE

1. Dress properly
Do not wear baggy shirts or swirling dresses to light a barbecue. They may catch fire.

2. Position the barbecue safely
The barbecue should be placed outside on firm and sheltered ground at least 10 feet (3 m) from the house and well away from overhanging bushes or trees, and long, dry grass.

3. Prepare the lighting material
Roll up several sheets of newspaper and twist into doughnut shapes. Place these in the base of the barbecue. Small twigs, dry grass (twisted into doughnuts) and brushwood will do as an alternative, or buy some firelighters.

4. Place the coal on top
Over the top of the newspaper doughnuts or firelighters, arrange the charcoals to a depth of around 4 inches (10 cm). Use less coal if starting the fire with twigs and brushwood.

5. Light the barbecue
Make sure any breeze is coming from behind you to stop smoke getting in your eyes or flames flaring up in your face. Use a taper or long match to light the newspaper / firelighters / brushwood *(a)*. Once alight, feed oxygen to the flames by blowing air onto the fire at the base.

a. Use a long match or taper to light the barbecue.

6. If the flames go out
Use tongs to remove the coals and place them in a fireproof container. Reapply lighting material and try again.

DO NOT

Throw flammable liquids, compost, bank statements or live animals onto a barbecue.

Leave a barbecue with a drunk person or someone easily distracted.

IDENTIFY STRENGTHS AND AREAS FOR IMPROVEMENT

Tick the correct score bubble:

	bad	fair	good	very good	excellent
Appropriate dress	0 1	2 3 4	5 6	7 8	9 10
Lighting technique	0 1	2 3 4	5 6	7 8	9 10
Standing around technique	0 1	2 3 4	5 6	7 8	9 10
Condition of sausages	0 1	2 3 4	5 6	7 8	9 10

Total score ——— **Evaluator** ———

Score: ★★★ 33–40 / ★★ 17–32.99 / ★ 5–16.99 / Try harder 0–4.99

WEEK 24

PLANTING A TUB OF MUSTARD AND CRESS

★

Time management is the key to mustard and cress cultivation. If aiming to have a mustard and cress salad garnish at your great aunt's tea party, you need to plant at least ten days in advance. The objective is to have a nutritious salad, tasty mustard and cress sandwiches, and your aunt's glowing approval.

You will need: empty margarine tub, packet of mustard and cress seeds, kitchen towel, cotton wool, plastic bag and twist tie, warm dark place, great aunt (optional)

TECHNIQUE

1. Clean out the margarine tub and prepare it for cultivation

Ten days before your aunt is due to visit, wash the tub thoroughly, place a layer of damp kitchen towel in the bottom, then a layer of cotton wool *(a)*. Sprinkle water on the cotton wool until it is moist all over.

2. Sow the cress seeds

The cress seeds should be sown about three days before the mustard seeds so they both mature at the same time. Sprinkle the seeds thickly onto the cotton wool, leaving some space for the mustard later. The seeds do not need to be covered; just press them down onto the cotton wool and make sure they are moist.

a. Prepare the tub with damp kitchen towel and cotton wool. Plant the seeds on top.

3. Put the seeds in a warm cupboard to germinate

Put the tub inside a plastic bag, seal with a twist tie, and place it inside a warm, dark cupboard to encourage the seeds to germinate.

4. Add the mustard seeds

Three days later, add the mustard seeds to the pot, making sure the cotton wool is still moist. Return the pot to the cupboard.

5. On the 7th or 8th day
When the seedlings are about 2 inches (5 cm) high, remove the pot from the cupboard, take it out of the plastic bag, and place it on a window sill. Turn the container daily for even growth, and keep it out of direct sunlight.

6. Harvest the crop
When the seedlings have turned a healthy green colour and are standing up strongly you can harvest them to eat in sandwiches or add to your salad bowl.

FOR HIGH FLYERS

★

Sow mustard and cress seeds at ten-day intervals for a salad crop throughout the year.

★

Experiment with mustard and cress cuisine.

IDENTIFY STRENGTHS AND AREAS FOR IMPROVEMENT
★
Ask your great aunt for an honest assessment:

	bad	fair	good	very good	excellent
Sowing technique	0 1	2 3 4	5 6	7 8	9 10
Germination success	0 1	2 3 4	5 6	7 8	9 10
Timing	0 1	2 3 4	5 6	7 8	9 10
Taste	0 1	2 3 4	5 6	7 8	9 10

Total score _____ **Evaluator** _____

Score: ★★★ 33–40 / ★★ 17–32.99 / ★ 5–16.99 / Try again 0–4.99

WEEK 25

ROLLING UP A SLEEPING BAG

★

Packing away a sleeping bag, with practice, and in the right conditions, can be done in just 30 seconds. If completing this task after a wet night, wait until the bag is dry before you roll it away – a soggy bag rolled up is unpleasant, likely to smell, and weighs more. If you have trouble with co-ordination, employ an assistant to help.

You will need: sleeping bag, waterproof compression sack, canvas sack for home storage, assistant (optional)

TECHNIQUE

1. Find a suitable place to roll up the sleeping bag
The ground should be flat, dry and free from undergrowth that might tear the bag. Short, springy grass is ideal.

2. Lay the bag out flat
Lay out the bag with its outer side facing the ground. If it is not zipped up, zip it up now.

3. Fold and roll
Fold the bag over lengthways and roll it up from the closed end, expelling air outwards as you roll *(a)*. Keep the roll as tight as possible; if necessary, kneel on the rolled portion every so often to make it tighter. Ask your assistant for help.

4. Insert into the compression sack
Keeping the roll tight with the help of your knees, take the compression sack and fit it over one end of the roll. Gently ease the sack down over the roll, all the time making sure the roll doesn't unwind. Once the whole roll is inside the sack, pull the drawstring tight and use the straps (if there are any) to further reduce the sleeping bag pack size. The compression sack will keep your bag dry.

5. If the bag doesn't fit into the sack
Start again.

a. Fold the sleeping bag lengthways and start rolling from closed end.

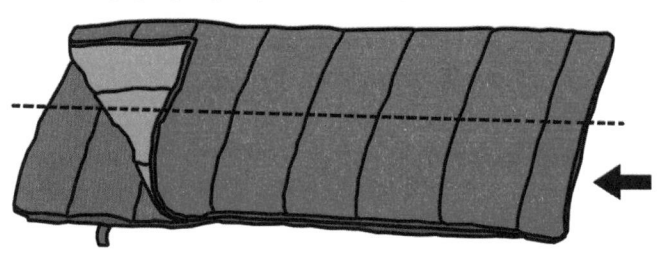

6. When home

Don't store your sleeping bag inside the compression sack for long periods of time because it will damage the insulation. Instead keep the bag rolled up loosely in a breathable canvas sack, and take it out every few months to fluff it up.

TIPS

★ Ask an assistant to help you keep the roll tight.

★ Check inside the sleeping bag before you roll it up.

IDENTIFY STRENGTHS AND AREAS FOR IMPROVEMENT

★

Tick the correct score bubble:

	bad	fair	good	very good	excellent
Rolling technique	0 1	2 3 4	5 6	7 8	9 10
Keeping roll tight with knees	0 1	2 3 4	5 6	7 8	9 10
Inserting roll in sack	0 1	2 3 4	5 6	7 8	9 10
Long-term storage	0 1	2 3 4	5 6	7 8	9 10

Total score _____   **Evaluator** _____

Score: ★★★ 33–40 / ★★ 17–32.99 / ★ 5–16.99 / Try harder 0–4.99

WEEK 26

COMPLAINING TO THE COUNCIL

★

Councils usually want to know when services have gone wrong and most will provide a formal complaint procedure. To make a successful complaint you must show how the council has failed in its services, and how this has directly affected you. You need to be persistent to get results.

You will need: something to complain about

TECHNIQUE

1. Which council or authority?
First find out which council or authority has responsibility for whatever it is you want to complain about. There may be separate authorities in your area responsible for housing, refuse collection, school organisation, etc.

2. Investigate the complaint procedure
Obtain complaint forms or contact names and addresses for sending a complaint letter. Don't wait too long before you send your complaint.

3. State your case
Make sure you explain what you think the council or authority has done wrong, or what it has failed to do, how it has affected you and what you think they must do to put things right *(a)*. You can't simply disagree with a council's decision or action; the council must have managed or administered something badly or dishonestly, and you must have suffered as a direct consequence.

4. Assess whether you are satisfied with the response
If the council or authority fails to rectify the error within a reasonable time, consider taking your complaint to a higher authority for investigation, for example, the local government ombudsman.

a. Craft your letter carefully.

HOW TO KNOW WHEN SERVICES HAVE GONE WRONG

TIPS

★

• Write legibly • Keep a copy • Date the letter • Address the official courteously

PERFORMANCE ASSESSMENT

★

Ask your MP for an honest assessment:

No reply for 6 months, meanwhile you forgot what you were complaining about	**1 point**
Acknowledgment received, reminders sent, matter resolved 2.5 years later	**10 points for persistence**
Apologetic response from council, matter rectified within 1 week, compensation received	**100 points plus medal**

WEEK 27

OPENING A TIN CAN

There are several ways to open a tin can, some of them dangerous. Avoid boy-scout methods using pen knives and pointed rocks. These usually end in injuries. A can opener is the correct tool, or use the pull-ring or key device that comes with the can. The objective is to get a clean-away top without spilling your peach halves in the process, and without causing yourself an injury.

You will need: tin can, tin opener, first-aid kit

TECHNIQUE

1. Sterilise the can opener
Drop the can opener into a pan of boiling water or run it under a hot tap if short of time.

2. Prepare the can for opening
Meticulously scrub the can before opening to avoid contamination of contents. Place the cleaned can on a firm table or countertop.

3. Apply the can opener to open the can
Fit the metal ridge of the can opener over the rim of the tin, with the butterfly crank handle pointing outwards. Press the arms of the can opener together, exterting downward pressure so the metal ridge punctures the can top. Holding the arms of the can opener in one hand, use the other to twist the butterfly handle until the opener has travelled the full circle of the top and the lid pops *(a)*.

4. Remove the lid
Taking care not to cut your fingers, remove the can lid *(b)*. If the lid doesn't pop first time, reapply the can opener. Do not attempt to pry open the can with a spoon.

a. Twist the handle until the lid pops open.

5. Opening a can with a ring-pull

If the can has a ring-pull, hold the can with one hand and use the other to lift the ring-pull to a vertical position. Pull the ring upwards and gently backwards until the lid comes clean off the tin *(c)*.

6. Opening a sardine can with a key

Remove the detachable key and thread the loose metal flap on the edge of the can into the looped end of the key. Turn the key slowly, peeling back the can lid until it pops off *(d)*. Take care not to spill the contents.

b. Remove the can lid, taking care not to cut yourself.

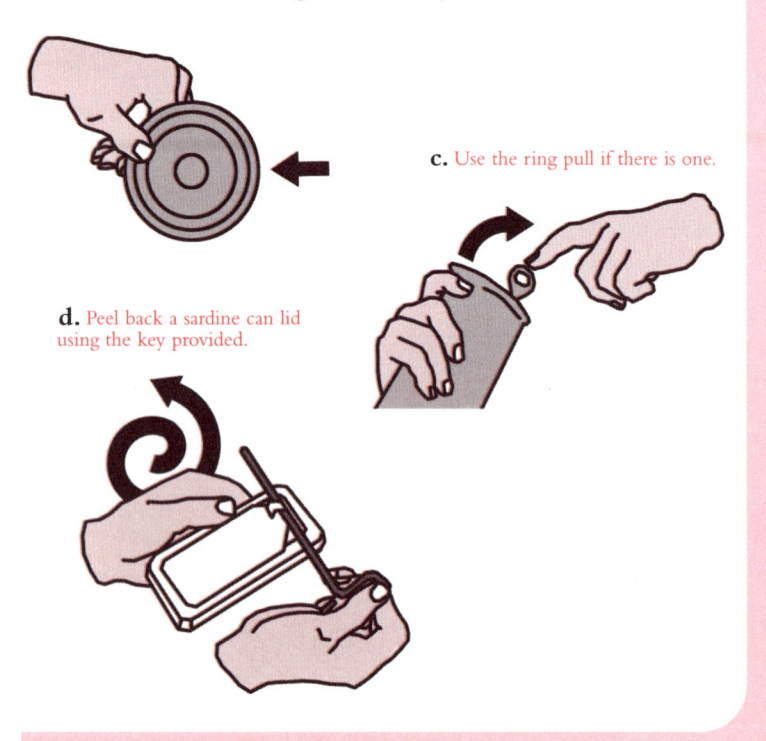

c. Use the ring pull if there is one.

d. Peel back a sardine can lid using the key provided.

NOT RECOMMENDED

★

Opening a can with a hammer and chisel is for life and death situations only.

PERFORMANCE ASSESSMENT

★

	can of soup (ring-pull)	can of peaches (can opener)	sardine can (key twist)
Lid pops off cleanly, no injuries	★★★	★★★	★★★
Hammer and screwdriver assistance	●	●	●
Hospitalisation required	● ●	● ●	● ●

Total score

1 ● or more: buy an electric can opener

3 ★ or more: good work

WEEK 28

IRONING A FRILLY BLOUSE

Always be prepared for the comeback of the frilly blouse. You may already have a frilly blouse (perhaps you played a part in *The Titanic* or you like 80s gear). If not, buy one as ironing it will hone your skills and save you money at the dry cleaners. The time allowed for ironing a frilly blouse is 20 minutes.

You will need: frilly blouse, iron, ironing board, sleeve board (optional)

TECHNIQUE

1. Set up the ironing board
For comfortable ironing, the board should be at hip height.

2. Prepare the iron
Check the label on the blouse for the recommended iron heat, turn on the iron and adjust the heat setting. If using a steam iron, add water from the kettle *(a)*. When the iron is hot, pass it over a light-coloured cloth to be sure of no soiling from the soleplate. Test the iron on a hidden piece of the blouse fabric. If it sizzles, the iron is too hot and should be adjusted.

3. Iron the frilly bits first
Lay the frill on the ironing board and smooth it flat. Iron on the reverse side, from the outer edge of the frill towards where it gathers. Use your fingers to keep the frill flat and stop creasing. If the fabric is raw silk, use a dry iron. If the frills are made of lace, or another delicate material, use a cloth between the iron and the lace, and apply a boost of steam. For embroidery, velvet and acrylics, place a towel on the ironing board beneath the garment to avoid creating sheen. Keep the temperature low and iron on the reverse.

a. Fill a steam iron with water from the kettle.

4. Iron the rest of the blouse
Use the narrow end of the board or a sleeve board to stop creases forming when you iron the shoulders and sleeves. Iron the cuffs on the inside and then the outside, and the same with the collar. Iron the body of the blouse beginning with one side and working round to the other.

5. Hang up the blouse

Hang the ironed blouse in a warm place where air can circulate and any dampness dry off. Do not cram it into an overcrowded closet.

TIP
★

Avoid circular motions that stretch the fabric.

WARNING
★

Never leave the iron unattended.

IDENTIFY STRENGTHS AND AREAS FOR IMPROVEMENT
★

Tick the correct score bubble:

	bad	fair	good	very good	excellent
Iron handling	0 1	2 3 4	5 6	7 8	9 10
Frills and ruffles	0 1	2 3 4	5 6	7 8	9 10
Shoulders and sleeves	0 1	2 3 4	5 6	7 8	9 10
Finished look	0 1	2 3 4	5 6	7 8	9 10

Total score _____ **Evaluator** _____

Score: ★★★ 33–40 / ★★ 17–32.99 / ★ 5–16.99 / Try again 0–4.99

WEEK 29

FEEDING A HEDGEHOG

★

Welcoming a hedgehog into your garden can bring considerable benefits. In just one night a hedgehog will eat half a tin full of insects, beetles, worms, snails and black slugs. Large orange-footed slugs tend to stick together a hedgehog's lips and are more difficult to digest, but there is no denying that hedgehogs are heroic controllers of many garden pests. The aim of this task is to encourage and reward them.

You will need: garden, slugs, dog or cat food, paving slabs, bricks, hedgehog

TECHNIQUE

1. Is your garden suitable for hedgehogs?
Cats usually respect hedgehogs but some dogs (for example, terriers) take advantage of their nice nature and bite them. Also beware steep-sided ponds: hedgehogs can topple into them while having a drink. Make a small ladder so they can climb out.

2. Hedgehog habits
To survive, a hedgehog needs ten large gardens full of grubs. Don't expect a hedgehog to stay in just one garden full-time.

3. Helping wild hedgehogs
To survive hibernation a hedgehog should weigh between 20 and 22 oz (570-625 g). Young hedgehogs born in late autumn weigh less than this and need help to survive the winter.

4. Make a hedgehog feeding station
Place a paving slab on four bricks (one at each corner) and put food under the slab where hedgehogs can reach it but cats and foxes can't *(a)*. Hedgehogs tend to put their noses under the rims of saucers and flip them over, so use a heavy flat dish.

a. A hedgehog feeding station can be made with a slab balanced on four bricks.

5. Hedgehog food
Hedgehogs like cat or dog food but not with fish. They particularly like turkey, chicken and rabbit flavours, and crunchy cat biscuits *(b)*. Or buy special hedgehog food from your local pet shop. Always provide water.

6. Hedgehog myths
Feeding hedgehogs bread and milk will do more harm than good, but baby hedgehogs can be fed goat's milk.

7. Treats
For the occasional special treat, feed crushed peanuts, biscuits, dried fruit or birthday cake.

b. Hedgehogs love cat food and crunchy cat biscuits. Always provide water.

HAZARDS

★

Check there are no hedgehogs under your bonfire before setting it alight.

★

Check long grass first before switching on your strimmer or hover mower.

★

Avoid forking the compost heap in winter when a family of hedgehogs might be hibernating inside.

WARNING SIGN

★

If you see a hedgehog out during a hot day, or lying uncurled with its legs in the air, it is in trouble. Contact a veterinary surgeon or hedgehog doctor immediately.

PERFORMANCE ASSESSMENT

★

	very good	try again	try harder	very bad
Hedgehogs keep coming back	●			
Hedgehogs disappear after one feed		●		
Hedgehog found in pond or locked in shed			●	
Hedgehog spines found in grass cuttings				●

WEEK 30

PUTTING UP A DECKCHAIR

★

The folding deckchair, icon of seaside resorts, cruise ships and summer sun, is rapidly disappearing from our beaches, parks and gardens, replaced by the cushioned lounger. Skills for erecting a deckchair are gradually being lost. The aim of this task is to resurrect the traditional deckchair, and to get one unfolded within 30 minutes, without injury.

You will need: traditional deckchair (no cushioned loungers)

TECHNIQUE

1. Dress sensibly
Wear shoes and cover any protruding body parts that might become caught in the wooden mechanism. Other than that, dress for the beach.

2. Lay the deckchair flat on the ground
Find a firm piece of ground and lay the deckchair frame flat, facing in the direction you want to be. The shorter outer frame (which will form the chair stay) should be unfolded and flat on the ground too. Its position indicates where the back of the chair will be *(a)*.

a. Lay the chair flat on the ground.

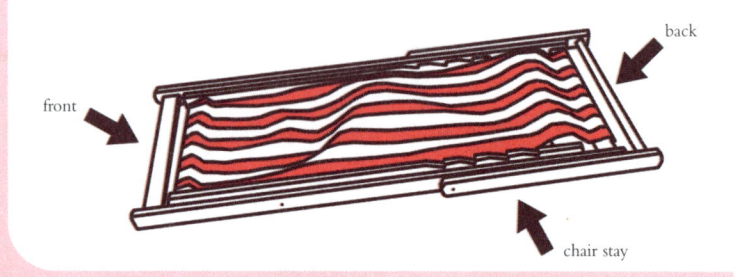

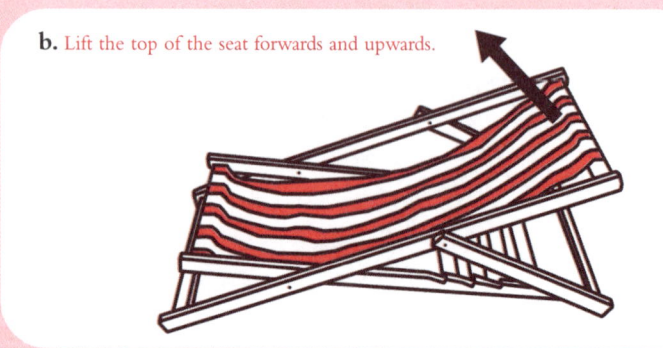

front — back — chair stay

b. Lift the top of the seat forwards and upwards.

3. Grab hold of the top of the seat
Pick up the top of the seat – the horizontal bar with canvas attached that lies inside the chair stay when the deckchair is flat *(b)*.

4. Lift upwards
Keeping hold of the same piece, gently lift the frame upwards. The chair stay will lift too and engage with the notches in the lower seat frame, securing the chair in an upright position.

5. Adjust the chair height
Deckchairs have three or more heights to choose from. Fit the chair stay into the top notch if you want to sit upright (appropriate for eating), the middle notch for a relaxed sitting position (appropriate for talking) or the bottom notch to recline (appropriate for sleeping) *(c)*.

c. Adjust the sitting position with the chair stay.

WARNING

★

Do not sit on a deckchair if *(a)* you haven't checked the mechanism for several years, or *(b)* you are overweight.

IDENTIFY STRENGTHS AND AREAS FOR IMPROVEMENT

★

Tick the correct score bubble:

	bad	fair	good	very good	excellent
Appropriate dress	0 1	2 3 4	5 6	7 8	9 10
Deckchair erection technique	0 1	2 3 4	5 6	7 8	9 10
Injury avoidance	0 1	2 3 4	5 6	7 8	9 10
Completion in reasonable time★	0 1	2 3 4	5 6	7 8	9 10

★ reasonable time suggested: 30 minutes

Total score ――――――― **Evaluator** ―――――――

Score: ★★★ 33–40 / ★★ 17–32.99 / ★ 5–16.99 / Buy a cushioned lounger 0–4.99

WEEK 31

ENDING AN AFFAIR

★

The aim of this task is not to end a long-term relationship – a serious and highly ambitious undertaking – but to break up from a casual liaison of a few weeks. For many people, this common, everyday occurrence is surprisingly difficult. Practising and perfecting the art of 'ending it' will save you a good deal of wasted time and effort.

You will need: casual fling, courage

TECHNIQUE

a. Arrange to meet in a public place.

1. Arrange to meet your lover
As soon as you realise the affair is going nowhere, telephone your lover and arrange to meet for a coffee during the day in a public place – preferably not your favourite haunt in case you want to return one day *(a)*.

2. Dress conservatively
Wear dull, business-like clothes. Avoid wearing a dress or suit that your lover particulary likes.

3. Get to the point
On arrival, offer a drink but don't get side-tracked with chit chat. Sum up why you thought you were attracted to your lover in the first place and how much you've enjoyed the last few weeks. Then explain that you've made a mistake. Announce that you've decided it would be best to finish the affair. Avoid adding that you hope to remain friends – unless you think this is really possible.

4. Leave quickly
Don't be persuaded to change your mind. Explain that you have to leave to meet your aunt. Don't say where she lives.

5. If the previous steps do not work
A lover who will not take your decision as final should be avoided at all costs. Do not answer their calls. If they arrive on your doorstep, do not invite them in. If necessary, explain your decision again and this time point out the things you don't like about them, especially the way they are harassing you. Finally, confess to meeting someone else.

LAST RESORT TACTICS

★

Tell your lover that he/she owes you money. • Burn her dresses/his shirts and send the ashes in a parcel. • Cast a spell to turn you into an ugly frog (in your lover's eyes). • Put your new lover's name on your answer machine. • Wear a false beard and big eyebrows. • Go on a 6-month vacation.

IDENTIFY STRENGTHS AND AREAS FOR IMPROVEMENT

★

Tick the correct score bubble:

	bad	fair	good	very good	excellent
Meeting place	0 1	2 3 4	5 6	7 8	9 10
'Ending it' speech	0 1	2 3 4	5 6	7 8	9 10
Avoidance of injury	0 1	2 3 4	5 6	7 8	9 10
Level of success	0 1	2 3 4	5 6	7 8	9 10

Total score Lover 1 _____ **Lover 2** _____ **Lover 3** _____

Score: ★★★ 33–40 / ★★ 17–32.99 / ★ 5–16.99 / Try last resort tactics 0–4.99

WEEK 32

REMOVING A SPLINTER

★

Removing a splinter fills most people with dread, but it needn't be so. With practice you can remove a splinter quickly, painlesslesly and without causing tissue damage or infection. It should take no more than 5 minutes. If the splinter is very large, deeply embedded, jagged or near to or in the eye, get professional medical help.

You will need: splinter (wood, glass, metal or thorn), candle or rubbing alcohol, needle, fine pair of tweezers, bandaid, antiseptic cream, soap and water, steady hand

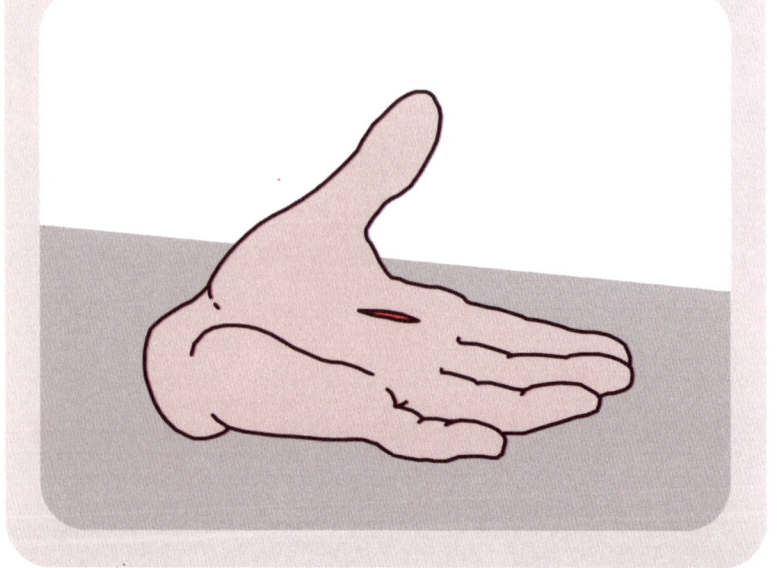

TECHNIQUE

1. Sterilize equipment and clean the wound
Wash the area around the splinter with warm water and soap. Sterilize the needle and tweezers by holding for 30 seconds in an open flame and allowing to cool *(a)*, or by immersing in rubbing alcohol and allowing to dry.

a. Sterilize the needle in an open flame.

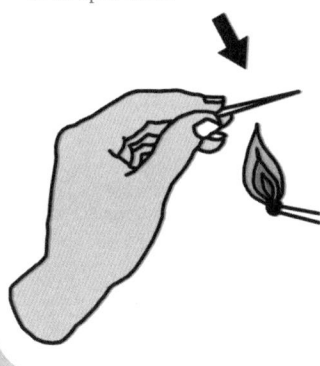

2. First try gentle teasing
By squeezing the skin on either side of the splinter, you may be able to ease it out enough to grab one end with the tweezers. If so, pull the splinter out gently but firmly in the direction it entered *(b)*.

b. Pull the splinter out in the direction it entered.

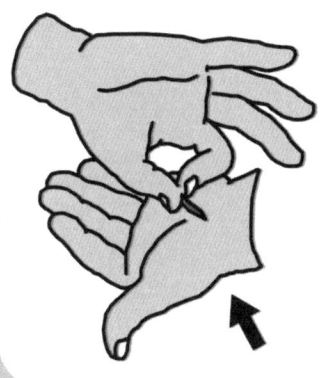

3. Use a needle
If the splinter head is not showing, use the needle to tear a small opening in the skin above the end of the splinter. Gently insert the closed tweezers into the hole. When they touch the splinter, open the tweezer grip slightly and close over the end of the splinter. Withdraw the tweezers and the splinter should come too.

4. Clean and dress the wound
Wash the wound with soap and water, and cover with a thin layer of antiseptic cream and a bandaid. If not up to date with your tetanus vaccines, go and have one in case of infection.

ALTERNATIVE TECHNIQUES

★

A splinter may come out if you stick a piece of parcel tape over it and pull.

★

A splinter may come out if you soak for long enough in a hot bath.

WARNING

★

Leaving half a splinter in your finger can lead to inflammation and infection.

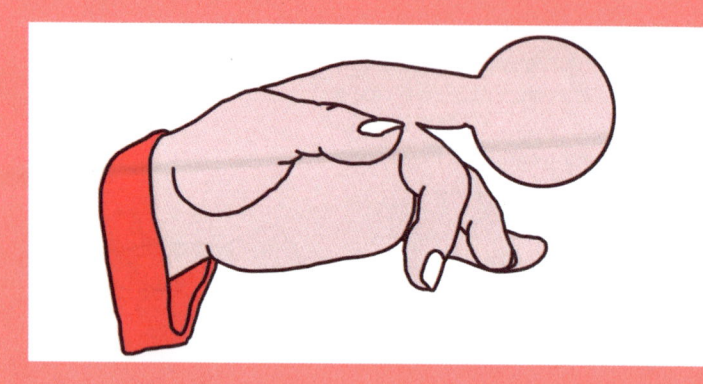

IDENTIFY STRENGTHS AND AREAS FOR IMPROVEMENT

★

Tick the correct score bubble:

	bad	fair	good	very good	excellent
Equipment sterilization	0 1	2 3 4	5 6	7 8	9 10
Needle technique	0 1	2 3 4	5 6	7 8	9 10
Wound dressing	0 1	2 3 4	5 6	7 8	9 10
Courage shown	0 1	2 3 4	5 6	7 8	9 10

Total score _____ **Evaluator** _____

Score: ★★★ 33–40 / ★★ 17–32.99 / ★ 5–16.99 / Get medical help 0–4.99

WEEK 33

ERECTING A THREE-MAN TENT

★

For camping to be an enjoyable outdoor experience, and not a miserable nightmare, erecting a tent should be simple, efficient and painless. The objective of this task is to erect a three-person tent (which is really a tent for two people with some extra space for bags, equipment, dog or cat) to an adequate standard within 5 minutes.

You will need: three-man tent, helper

TECHNIQUE

1. Before you leave
Check you have all equipment: inner tent, fly sheet, groundsheet, poles, pegs, guylines, wooden hammer (or a rock), torch, assembly instructions.

2. Find a place to pitch the tent
Choose a flat, well drained area, free from rocks, sharp objects and ants. If you have a separate waterproof groundsheet, lay it out on the site.

3. Position the tent
Unfold the inner tent and spread it out, with the door in the correct position. Secure with tent pegs hammered through the loops around the edge of the tent.

4. Assemble the poles
A dome tent, now a highly popular design of tent, has bendy poles made up of jointed, cord-attached pieces that slot together. The two main poles cross diagonally to each corner of the tent. Under tension they bend upwards and form the dome. A shorter pole forms the framing for the verandah.

5. Insert the poles into the pole sleeves
Locate one of the pole sleeves that passes diagonally over the middle of the tent and push a main pole through the sleeve, taking care not to rip the fabric. Repeat with the other pole and sleeve.

6. Create the dome
At each corner of the tent, insert the end of the pole into a special grommet (or if there is a metal key, insert the key into the hollow end of the pole). To fit the poles into the grommets requires some force and the tension will cause the poles to bend, forming the dome in the middle of the tent.

7. Finish off
Peg out the guylines for the inner tent, spread the flysheet over the top of the dome, with the door in the correct place, and

peg all round. If you have a verandah, peg it out in front of the tent, insert a pole into the pole sleeve and secure with guylines. Pull all guylines taut.

WINDY WEATHER WARNING

★

Secure the tent with extra pegs.

IDENTIFY STRENGTHS AND AREAS FOR IMPROVEMENT

★

Ask a person on your campsite to give an honest assessment:

	bad	fair	good	very good	excellent
Inner tent	0 1	2 3 4	5 6	7 8	9 10
Poles	0 1	2 3 4	5 6	7 8	9 10
Pegs	0 1	2 3 4	5 6	7 8	9 10
Flysheet	0 1	2 3 4	5 6	7 8	9 10

Total score ——— **Evaluator** ———

Score: ★★★ 33–40 / ★★ 17–32.99 / ★ 5–16.99 / Try a B&B 0–4.99

WEEK 34

TAKING A SIESTA

★

Most people are affected by mid-afternoon sleepiness, especially after lunch. The purpose of this task is to adopt the civilized Spanish-Mexican tradition of taking a siesta, or afternoon nap. It takes organisation and negotiation skills to fit a siesta into a modern working schedule. The benefits are improved attention, concentration, efficiency and memory.

You will need: sympathetic boss, dark room with bed / trees with hammock, alarm clock

TECHNIQUE

1. Notice when you get sleepy
Most people find the hours between 3 and 5 p.m. are the worst for drowsiness *(a)*.

2. Arrange your siesta
This may involve convincing your boss that productivity will greatly improve if you can be allowed a nap *(b)*. Work late to make up time if necessary.

3. Power nap
A 'power nap' lasting 10 minutes will give you 10 minutes of non-REM (rapid eye movement) sleep, allowing some physical

a. Check what time you get sleepy.

b. Convince your boss that productivity will rise if you take a siesta.

restoration in a short space of time. Try and squeeze an extra five minutes to give you time to fall asleep.

4. Find a suitable place to sleep
Look for a dark, quiet room with a comfortable bed or sofa, or a hammock in a shady place if you sleep better outside. Failing that, bring a roll-up mat and find an empty office or broom cupboard. As a last resort, put a 'do not disturb' notice on the door, take the phone off the hook and lay your head on the desk in front of you.

5. The family snooze
Aim to negotiate a 3-hour afternoon break, allowing time to go home, eat with the family and sleep with your wife or husband, returning to work until 9 or 10 at night *(c)*. This traditional type of siesta will give you a cycle of non-REM sleep followed by a cycle of REM sleep (REM sleep brings full mental repair, and dreams).

c. Set your alarm to ring when you need to return to work.

FOR HIGH FLYERS

★

Work mornings only or a three-day week.

IF YOUR BOSS SAYS 'NO'

★

Put on 'wide-awake' glasses after lunch so you can snooze at your desk undetected.

★

Schedule in regular 2-5 p.m. 'meetings' when you can disappear to the park.

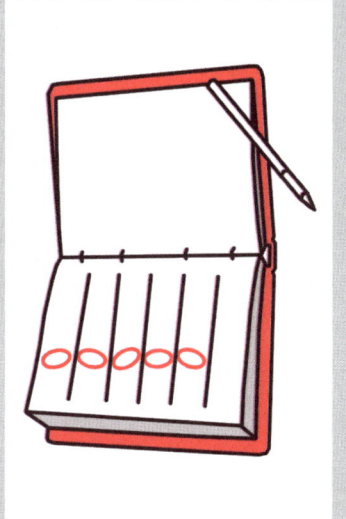

IDENTIFY STRENGTHS AND AREAS FOR IMPROVEMENT

★

Tick the correct box and fill in the productivity score for each day of the week:
Productivity poor: 0/1   fair: 2/3/4   good: 5/6   very good: 7/8   excellent: 9/10

	Monday	Tuesday	Wednesday	Thursday	Friday
10-minute nap	☐	☐	☐	☐	☐
3-hour break	☐	☐	☐	☐	☐
Productivity level					

Total weekly score _____   **Which day was best?** _____

WEEK 35

PREPARING FOR A CHEMICAL ATTACK

★

Being properly prepared in case of a chemical or gas attack is reassuring in times of potential terrorist action. Unlike an attack involving the release of a biological agent, which could take hours, even weeks, to detect, a chemical explosion is immediately visible. You need a fullproof plan of how to respond quickly in such an emergency.

You will need: disaster kit

TECHNIQUE

1. Devise an emergency plan
Make sure all family members know how to make contact and where to meet in case you cannot return to your home. Having an out-of-town rendez-vous and telephone or email contact point, for example a relative's home in the country, is advisable in case the town is evacuated.

2. Put together a disaster kit
In an easily transportable bag, include first aid supplies, a battery-powered radio and torch, spare batteries, a mobile telephone with battery charger, dense cotton fabric for covering your mouth and nose (for example, a folded T-shirt) or a close-fitting face mask, clothes, sleeping bag, bottled water, tinned or dried food, soap, special medications and other specific requirements, tools, maps and compass, cash and credit cards, useful telephone numbers and addresses, copies of passports, birth certificates and other important documents *(a)*.

3. Make additional copies of certificates and keep safely
Keep copies of important documents – birth certificates, wills, passport, etc – at a different address, for example, the home of a relative living out of town, or in a safe deposit box.

4. Check on emergency arrangements at work and school
For all family members, find out the emergency arrangements and emergency numbers at places of work and schools.

5. Be prepared at home
For situations where authorities advise you to stay in your home, have an interior room prepared as a shelter, preferably with a secure door and without windows. For situations where you are advised to leave the area and avoid breathing in a dangerous chemical, have in mind several easily accessible places in different directions where you can find clean air quickly, upwind of noxious fumes. In all situations, you will

need to know how to tune in to a radio or TV station for advice about safety and decontamination procedures.

6. Find out more

Learn to detect possible signs of chemical attack (choking, breathing difficulties, watery eyes, sick animals). Find out where to seek emergency medical attention in case of exposure and who you should contact if you detect anything suspicious. Research the official advice provided by appropriate authorities. Know how to turn off the water, gas and electricity supplies in your home. Learn the basics of first aid.

a. Prepare a disaster kit in case of emergency.

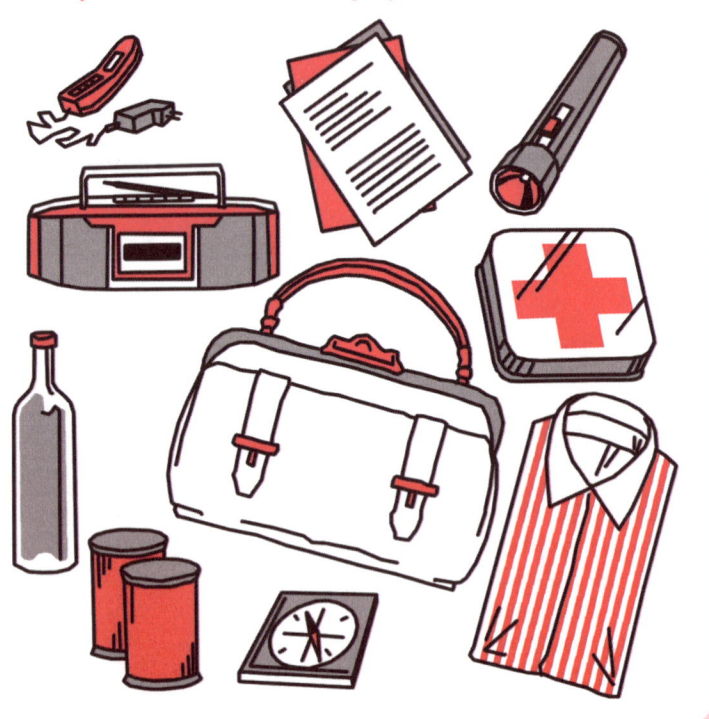

ADVICE FOR PARANOID PEOPLE

★

Wear a gas mask at all times.

ADVICE FOR NORMAL PEOPLE

★

Stay calm • Avoid disaster movies • Learn a language

PERFORMANCE ASSESSMENT

★

House sealed with tape, never go out	**Impractical**
Sold up, moved to Shetland Islands	**Okay if you like small ponies**
Sensible emergency plan	**On the right track**

121

WEEK 36

PUTTING UP A HEM

★

Hems are always falling down so you should easily find one to put up. The aim is not a quick fix with packing tape, staples, safety pins or giant paper clips, but to produce a neatly turned edge, even on all sides, that will stay up in most situations.

You will need: garment for hemming, pins, needle and thread, cotton, scissors, iron, assistant

TECHNIQUE

1. Determine the position of the hem
Put on the dress or trousers and get your assistant to pin up the hem to the required length.

2. Cut off excess material
Take off the garment and check the turn-up is straight, adjusting the pins where necessary. Cut off excess material, making sure you have at least 3 inches (8 cm) for the hem *(a)*.

3. Fold the hem
Working with the garment inside out, fold the end of the material under itself twice, half an inch (1 cm) at a time, so the raw edge is encased inside to stop it unravelling. With the iron switched on low heat, lightly press the hem where it turns up, and very lightly pass the iron over the double fold you have just made.

4. Sew the hem
Select appropriately coloured cotton thread, cut a piece 16–18 inches (40-45 cm) long, make a knot and thread the needle *(b)*.

a. When trimming excess material, leave a minimum of 3 inches (8 cm) for the hem.

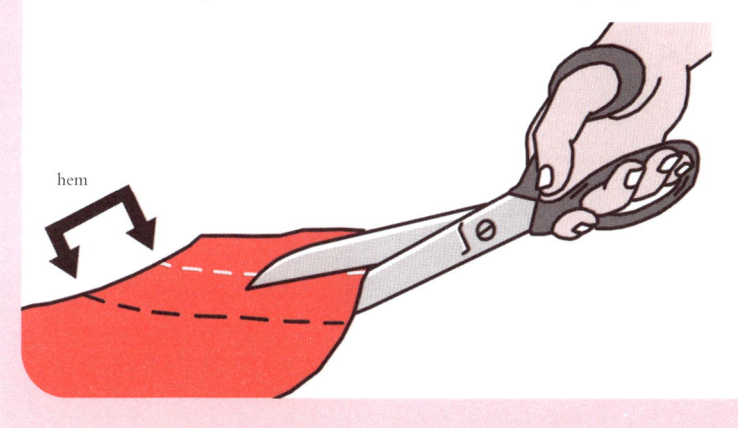

b. Use thread that matches the garment.

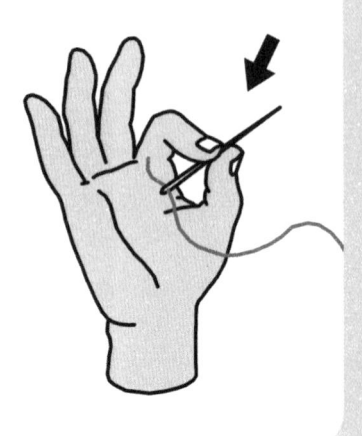

Stitch along the top of the hem using a running stitch as follows: slip the needle through the hem fold, then through the garment, picking up just one thread on the inside (so the stitching doesn't show on the outside), then back through the hem fold, and so on, with stitches less than half an inch (1 cm) apart. Secure every 6 inches (15 cm) with a few extra stitches into the hem fold so if your hem falls down it won't unravel all the way round.

5. Press the garment

Finally, press the bottom of the hem using a wet handkerchief between the hem and the iron. Avoid pressing the top of the hem if you don't want the hem outline to show through to the front of the garment.

ALTERNATIVE TECHNIQUES

★

Use iron-on tape instead of a needle and thread.

★

Use vertical velcro strips on the inside of the garment for a hem that moves up (or down) with fashion.

FOR HIGH FLYERS

★

Put up a ruffled chiffon hem on a ballroom dance costume (fishing line is recommended).

PERFORMANCE ASSESSMENT

★

Iron-on tape, competently applied	**10 points**
Needle and thread, invisible stitching	**25 points**
Ruffled chiffon hem with fishing line	**50 points**

WEEK 37

AVOIDING HOOLIGANS

★

Hooligans, miscreants, thugs and foul-mouthed delinquents are becoming increasingly evident. Learn to recognise the sound of yobs kicking your gate or your car, hurling abuse at old ladies or creating havoc upstairs on the bus. As soon as you spot them, take steps to avoid confrontation.

You will need: group of loutish young men and women.

TECHNIQUE

1. Be aware of trouble spots
Avoid places where gangs of hooligans hang out. If you have to go near them, try not to go alone and don't carry expensive looking hi-fi or telephone equipment or wear flashy jewellery.

2. Take purposeful steps to avoid confrontation
If you spot potential troublemakers ahead, avoid them by crossing the street *(a)*. Act as if you'd planned to go the other way. Head towards a well lit and busy area.

3. Avoid a verbal exchange
Refuse to get drawn into a conversation with a group of thugs. Throwing a rude comment or sign, or even looking in their direction, should be avoided too.

a. Cross to the other side of the street if you see a group of thugs.

4. Avoid violent encounters
If the local hoodlums look more like dangerous street fighters, and they approach aggressively, don't try out your martial arts moves. Run for help.

5. Report trouble to police
Give the authorities as much detail as possible. Be sure to distinguish between harmless teenage pranks and genuine anti-social behaviour or criminal activity.

UNDERCOVER HOODLUM

★

You may feel safer to become a hoodlum yourself – remember to look rough, carry beer and walk around with similar types.

WEAPONS WARNING

★

Disable hooligan traps when expecting visitors.

HOW DID YOU DO?

★

Bruised all over, broken arm and leg, cuts on knuckles	0 points
Organised a church hall tea party for hooligans; well attended, no trouble	100 points

WEEK 38

APPLYING NAIL VARNISH TO TOES

★

Paint your toenails for a feminine, summery look. Pick a colour to match your outfit, use toe dividers to avoid smudging, and do not be tempted to paint your nails at the last minute before leaving the house. Always remove polish before it starts to fade and chip.

You will need: nail clipper, emery board, bowl of warm water, towel, nail polish, base coat polish, clear varnish, cotton wool, cotton buds, cuticle conditioner, nail polish remover

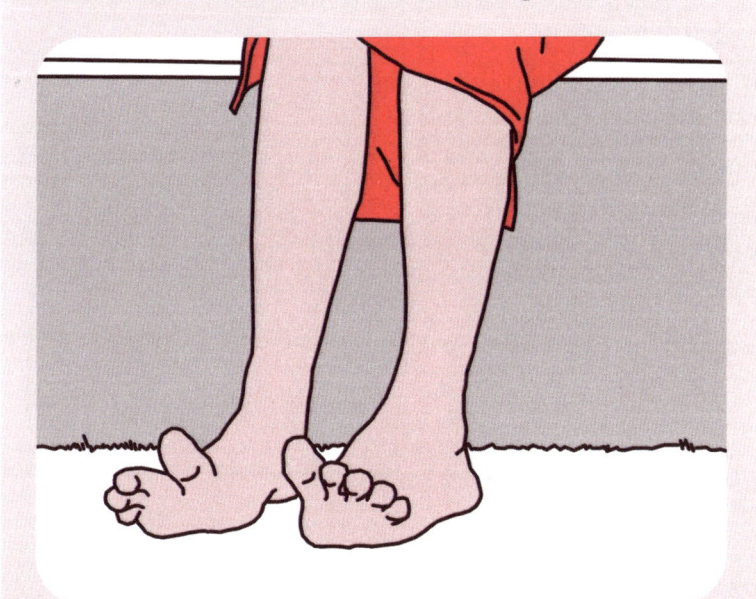

TECHNIQUE

1. Cut nails
Use a nail clipper to cut each toenail straight across (never shape nails as this can cause ingrowing toenails). Smooth sharp edges with an emery board *(a)*.

2. Remove old polish and wash feet
In a ventilated room, remove old polish using a cotton bud and nail polish remover. Soak your feet in a bowl of warm water, dry with a towel and apply cuticle conditioner at the base of each nail, gently pushing back the cuticle with a cotton bud. Clean off any excess with cotton wool.

3. Insert toe dividers
Place sufficient cotton wool between each toe to separate them. This will help to stop the polish from smudging.

4. Apply base coat
Avoid shaking the bottle of base coat and creating air bubbles; instead stir the liquid around a few times with the applicator. Apply one layer of base coat (or clear nail polish), covering each nail with three even strokes from the base of the nail to the top.

5. Apply nail polish
Make sure the base coat is fully dry before applying a coloured nail polish. Apply two layers, allowing the polish to dry in between each layer.

a. First cut your toenails.

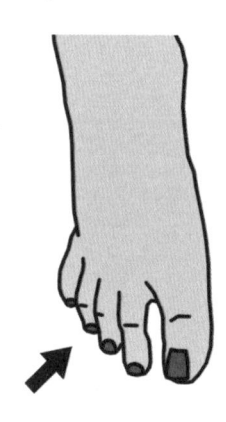

6. Apply top coat

When the second coloured layer is dry, apply a protective top coat of clear nail polish. Make sure the polish is dry before removing the toe dividers.

TIP

★

Toe dividers should be removed before leaving the house.

★

Calluses, corns, dry yellow skin, smashed or ingrown nails, mould, warts and blisters can spoil the effect of your nail polish.

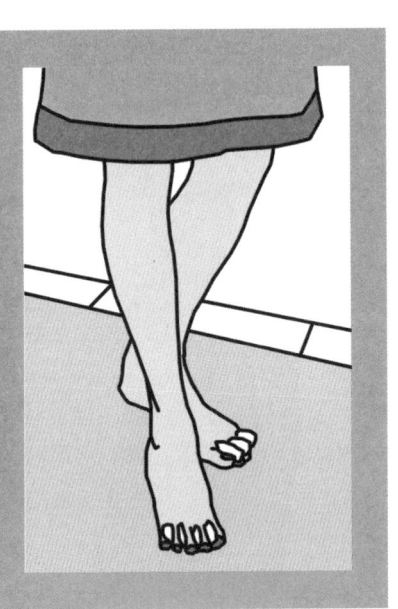

IDENTIFY STRENGTHS AND AREAS FOR IMPROVEMENT

★

Ask a boyfriend/girlfriend to give an honest assessment:

	bad	fair	good	very good	excellent
Nail trimming	0 1	2 3 4	5 6	7 8	9 10
Polish application	0 1	2 3 4	5 6	7 8	9 10
Use of toe dividers	0 1	2 3 4	5 6	7 8	9 10
Foot appeal	0 1	2 3 4	5 6	7 8	9 10

Total score ——— **Evaluator** ———

Score: ★★★ 33–40 / ★★ 17–32.99 / ★ 5–16.99 / Get a professional pedicure 0–4.99

WEEK 39

CLEANING A TOILET BOWL

There are no short cuts to properly cleaning a toilet. Find one that has an air of neglect and transform it to a standard of hygiene acceptable to the most discerning of visitors. It's dangerous work so wear appropriate protection and wash clothes immediately afterwards.

You will need: rubber gloves, eye goggles and nose mask, disinfectant, toilet cleaning solution, toilet brush, pumice stone, hand mirror, disposable cloth

TECHNIQUE

1. Open windows and doors
Before starting work, make sure there is plenty of ventilation.

2. Preparation
Put on rubber gloves and goggles. Lift the toilet seat. Lower the water level in the bowl by turning the toilet water supply off and flushing the toilet *(a)*.

3. Disinfect all areas
Use a spray disinfectant on all surfaces, including the seat, upper part of the toilet and handle. Leave for 10 minutes.

4. Apply toilet bowl cleaner and start cleaning
Make sure the cleaning solution covers all sides of the bowl and leave on for the recommended amount of time for the

a. Lift the toilet seat and lower the water level in the bowl.

product you are using *(b)*. Then, with cleaner liberally applied to the toilet brush, start swabbing beneath the rim and all round the bowl.

5. Remove stains
Pay particular attention to stains, including ring marks around the bowl, applying extra cleaner where necessary. Use a hand mirror to check for stains under the rim.

6. Flush and wipe down
Turn the water back on and flush the toilet while holding the toilet brush under the water to clean it. Use a disposable cloth for a final wipe down everywhere with disinfectant. Do not use the toilet until the disinfectant is dry.

b. The cleaning solution should cover all sides of the bowl.

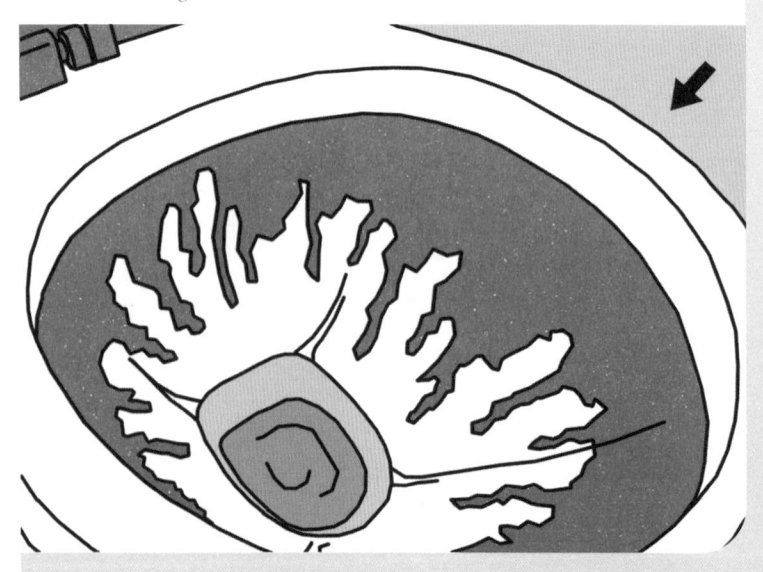

WARNING

★

Toilet bowl cleaner is not for human or animal consumption.

FOR THE INTREPID

★

Shift tough stains using a wet pumice stone.

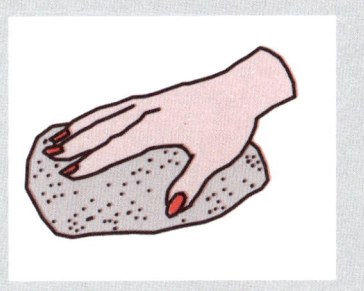

PERFORMANCE ASSESSMENT

★

Ask a visiting aunt to give an honest assessment:

Try harder	Yellow stain, brown marks still visible	1 point
★★★	Clean, bright and sweet-smelling	100 points

WEEK 40

LOOKING AFTER A NYLON STOCKING

★

Sheer stockings can make mottled, ripply legs look like blemish-free wonder limbs. They also go fabulously with garters, basques, corsets and panty girdles. But stockings are vulnerable garments that ladder in a split second and need careful looking after. Learn to handle them correctly, and if necessary change the way you sit, the bags you carry and how you get into a car.

You will need: pair of sheer stockings, suspender belt, bottle of clear nail varnish, hosiery gloves, talcum powder

TECHNIQUE

1. Preparation
If you have just had a shower, dry your legs thoroughly and apply some talcum powder. Make sure your toenails are trimmed and filed smooth. Put on a pair of hosiery gloves to avoid tearing the stocking with your nails *(a)*.

2. Put on the hosiery
Sitting on the edge of a soft furnishing – a bed or a comfortable sofa – bunch up the stocking with your thumbs inside the open end, place over your toes and gently ease the fabric up your leg. Fasten the broad band of fabric at the top to the catches of the suspender belt, one at the front and one at the outer side of your leg. Repeat with the other stocking.

a. Put on a pair of hosiery gloves to protect the stocking from your nails.

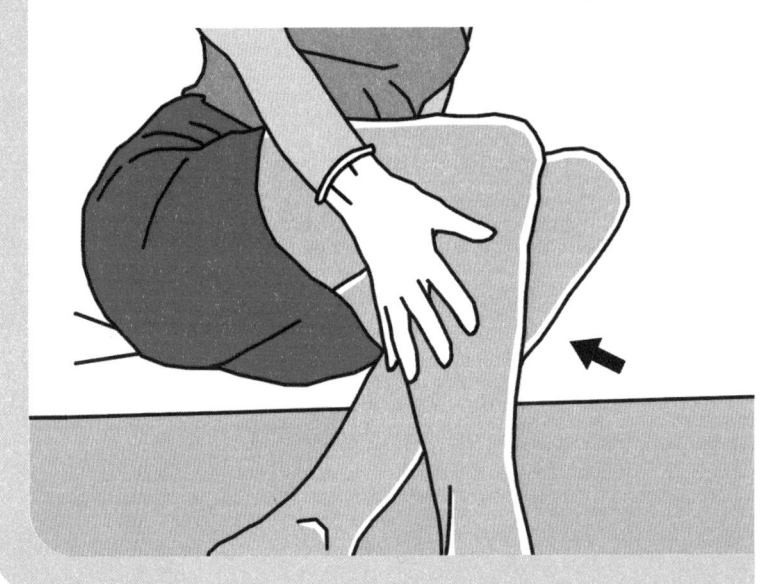

3. Ensure a good fit
Stockings are less vulnerable to damage if they fit perfectly so make sure they are not uncomfortably twisted by the suspender fastenings, stretched too tight, or loose and wrinkled around your ankles.

b. Keep your legs as straight as possible after detecting a hole.

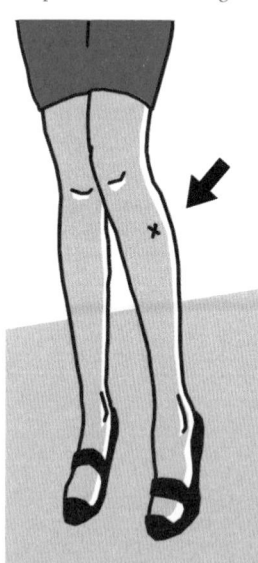

4. Be aware of where you put your legs
Once inside your hosiery you should take on a new attitude towards your legs, treating them like works of art that must not be scratched.

5. What to do if you see a small hole in your stocking
Keeping your legs as straight as possible, make your way to a discreet corner where you can take out the bottle of clear varnish *(b)*. The more movement you make the more likely the ladder is to run so don't go too far. Apply a small amount of varnish at either end of the developing hole. Do not move until the varnish is dry.

6. Carry a spare stocking at all times
If you cannot save the stocking, at least you will have a replacement.

RECYCLING AN OLD STOCKING

★ Salad dryer ★ Bank robber

PERFORMANCE ASSESSMENT
★

	1st day	2nd day	3rd day
Ladder in stocking	0 points	20 points	60 points
Hole mended	10 points	120 points	500 points

Date first worn _____ Date destroyed _____
Total points _____

WEEK 41

MAKING A ROCKERY ON A WINDOW SILL

★

The goal of small gardening is to create a naturalistic setting that hides its artificial origins, and to give an impression of distances, depths and realistic scale. The ultimate challenge in small gardening is to create an inside rockery on a window sill. You will develop nimble fingers, patience and a peaceful oasis where your imagination can roam freely.

You will need: deep-sided tray, potting compost, saucer, water sprinkler, moss, rockery plants, rocks, carrot tops, cocktail sticks, fuse wire

TECHNIQUE

1. Prepare a tray
Find a deep-sided tray, one that will fit on your window sill. Fill it nearly to the top with fine potting compost. Keep the compost damp.

2. Add a water feature
Sink a saucer lined with moss into the compost and fill with water. Place carrot tops in the water. After a few days, the carrots will look like miniature palm trees with fern sprouting from the top.

3. Arrange the rocks
Collect some interestingly shaped rocks and stones and create a careful grouping of them round the water feature. Pile them higher at one point to create a miniature mountain *(a)*.

a. Choose interestingly shaped rocks and create a miniature mountain.

4. Plant rockery plants
In the compost, plant miniature ferns, heathers and other small alpine plants with low-spreading foliage and tiny flowers.

5. Add a focal point
This could be an arbour made by binding cocktail sticks together using thin fuse wire, with a creeping plant growing over it, or a miniature Japanese temple . . .

TIP

★

Include the gnomes from your Christmas cake decoration set.

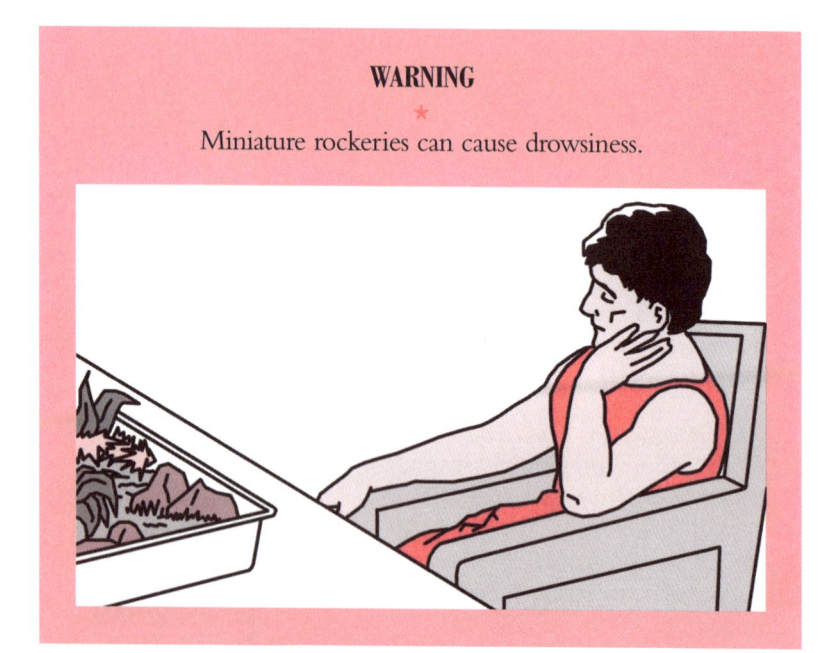

WARNING

★

Miniature rockeries can cause drowsiness.

IDENTIFY STRENGTHS AND AREAS FOR IMPROVEMENT

★

Tick the correct score bubble:

	bad	fair	good	very good	excellent
Naturalistic impression	0 1	2 3 4	5 6	7 8	9 10
Realistic scaling	0 1	2 3 4	5 6	7 8	9 10
Use of ornament	0 1	2 3 4	5 6	7 8	9 10
Overall beauty	0 1	2 3 4	5 6	7 8	9 10

Total score ———— **Evaluator**

Score: ★★★ 33–40 / ★★ 17–32.99 / ★ 5–16.99 / Try harder 0–4.99

WEEK 42

HANGING A PATTERNED WALLCOVERING

★

The aim in hanging a patterned wallcovering is for the pattern to look continuous around the room. On each adjacent length of paper the pattern should match up as closely as possible. Choose a large pattern to practise planning and positioning skills. Make sure the pattern is not cut in half at prominent places, for example, at the centre of the chimney breast.

You will need: wallpaper (unpasted), wallpaper paste, metal tape measure, plumb line, pasting brush, paper-hanging brush, pencil, scissors, clean cloth, long workbench, dust cloth, ladder

TECHNIQUE

1. Prepare the walls
Remove the old wallpaper, fill holes and apply a lining paper if the wallcovering requires one or if the plaster is old and porous.

2. Cut the first length of wallpaper
Unroll the new paper and check that the pattern is the right way up and the different rolls match in colour and quality. If the room has a chimney breast, plan to begin papering with a large pattern motif at the centre of this feature; otherwise, start near the door. Hang a plumb line, measure the height of the wall parallel to this line and cut the first length of wallpaper allowing 2 inches (5 cm) extra at top and bottom. Mark on the wall the position of this first piece and then calculate the number of lengths needed to cover all the walls.

a. Cut lengths of wallpaper to match the first length.

3. Cut the remaining lengths
Lay the first cut length on the workbench with the pattern side upwards. Unroll another piece and lay it beside the first, sliding it up or down until the patterns match, then cut top and bottom to the same length *(a)*. Repeat until you have cut all the lengths needed. On the reverse of each length mark the top with a 'T' and number them in the order they are to be hung.

4. Soak the first lengths in wallpaper paste
Use the pasting brush to spread an even coat of paste on the reverse of the first four lengths of wallpaper *(b)*. As each length

b. Paste the reverse side of each length of paper.

c. Smooth the paper onto the wall.

is pasted, gently fold over the top and bottom so the pasted surfaces meet in the middle (take care not to crease the paper). Leave the paper to absorb the paste (check manufacturer's instructions for optimum soaking time).

5. Hang the first length

Unfold and stick the top half of the first length on the position you marked on the wall earlier, aligning the paper with the plumb line. Use the paperhanging brush to smooth the paper onto the wall, working from the centre to remove trapped air *(c)*. Open up the bottom fold and smooth the lower part into place. With a pencil, mark the extra paper at top and bottom and cut away the excess.

6. Hang remaining lengths

Using the plumb line each time, hang the remaining lengths round the room, sliding them into position to align the pattern. When papering corners, measure and cut the length vertically so it reaches just around the corner (allowing extra for uneven walls), then cover over this margin with the adjoining length on the adjacent wall.

FOR HIGH FLYERS

★

Apply wallcovering round windows and doors.

TIP

★

Keep all offcuts for reuse later.

IDENTIFY STRENGTHS AND AREAS FOR IMPROVEMENT

★

Tick the correct score bubble:

	bad	fair	good	very good	excellent
Wall preparation	0 1	2 3 4	5 6	7 8	9 10
Cutting and pasting	0 1	2 3 4	5 6	7 8	9 10
Paper hanging	0 1	2 3 4	5 6	7 8	9 10
Pattern matching	0 1	2 3 4	5 6	7 8	9 10

Total score ———— **Evaluator** ————

Score: ★★★ 33–40 / ★★ 17–32.99 / ★ 5–16.99 / Employ a decorator 0–4.99

WEEK 43

DEALING WITH FACIAL HAIR

★

Unwanted facial hair on men is usually removed by shaving. On women and transsexuals, shaving causes hair to grow back even thicker than before and the stubble that quickly appears is usually considered unacceptable. Luckily, an unwanted moustache, chin hairs or sideburns can be removed by other methods, permanent and non-permanent. The purpose of this task is to discover the best one for you.

You will need: unwanted facial hair

TECHNIQUE

1. Shaving
If using a blade, wet the hair and apply plenty of shaving cream, gel or soap to help the blade glide smoothly. Keep the blade at a 30 degree angle, and when finished splash your face with cold water to stop any bleeding. For electric shaves, hold the skin and apply the shaver in the direction of hair growth.

a. Use tweezers to pluck out hairs from awkward places.

2. Waxing
This method pulls the hair out from the root and will last 1-2 months before you have to do it again. The hairs on your face need to be long enough to stick to the wax; it is also painful and can cause skin irritation so try a test area first. Apply the warm wax in the direction of hair growth. When removing, pull the cotton strip back in one smooth, fast operation.

3. Using tweezers
This also pulls the hair out from the root but is very painful and can cause sore skin. Use to remove just a few hairs from awkward places *(a)*.

4. Bleaching
This disguises the unwanted hair and is a cheap and easy method, though it can cause irritation to sensitive skin.

5. Applying a depilatory cream
These creams affect the hair root making the hair fall out or grow more slowly. They can cause itching and burning so should be applied to a test area first. Follow the product instructions and the guidance of a doctor or pharmacist.

6. Permanent hair removal

Electrolysis is a permanent hair removal technique involving the application of an electrical current to destroy the root of the hair. It is usually more reliable than laser hair removal for a permanent result. Both are costly and advice from a doctor, family and friends is advisable beforehand.

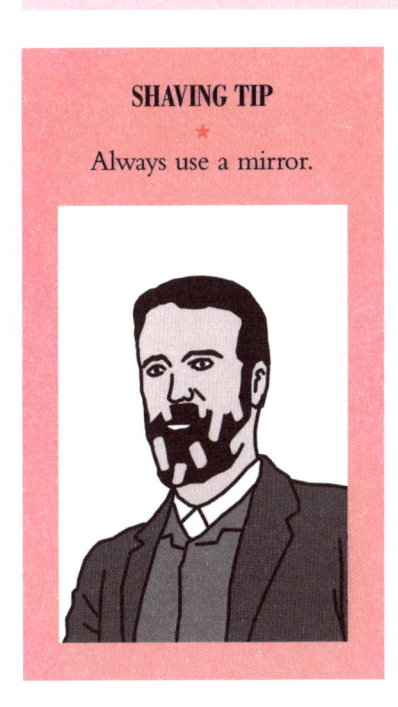

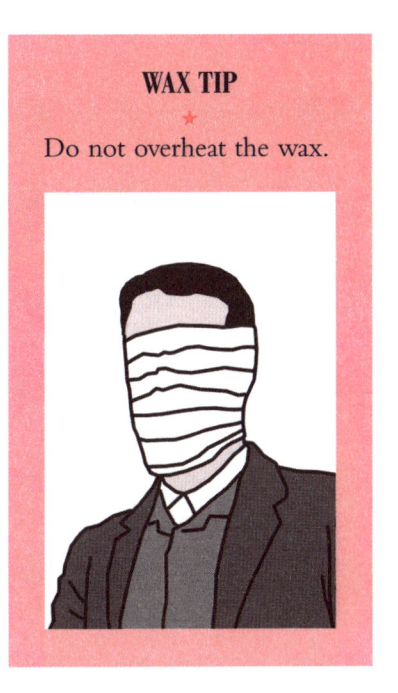

SHAVING TIP
★
Always use a mirror.

WAX TIP
★
Do not overheat the wax.

PERFORMANCE ASSESSMENT
★

Face after treatment:

Silky smooth	10 points
Sharp and stubbled	4 points
Red and hairy	2 points

WEEK 44

CHANGING A NAPPY

★

Finding a baby that needs a nappy change should be simple if you are a parent, grandparent, uncle or aunt, or a kind and helpful friend. The aim is to change a terry nappy – the washable type that doesn't clog up land-fill sites, unlike disposables. The final garment should stay on, and with good folding should stop any leaks.

You will need: baby, clean terry nappy, safety pin, nappy cover (optional), nappy bucket, baby wipes

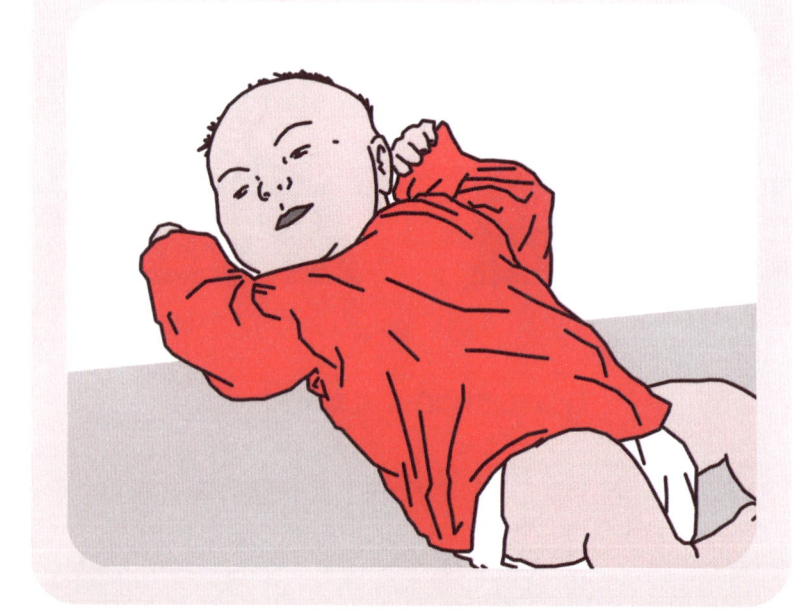

TECHNIQUE

151

1. Prepare a clean nappy

First wash your hands before folding the nappy. For a traditional kite fold, spread the nappy flat with one corner towards you. Fold the sides (*1*) and (*2*) so they meet at the centre *(a)*. Fold over the top corner (*3*) so the nappy is kite shaped *(b)*. Fold up the corner (*4*) facing you *(c)*.

a. Fold *(1)* and *(2)* so they meet at the centre.

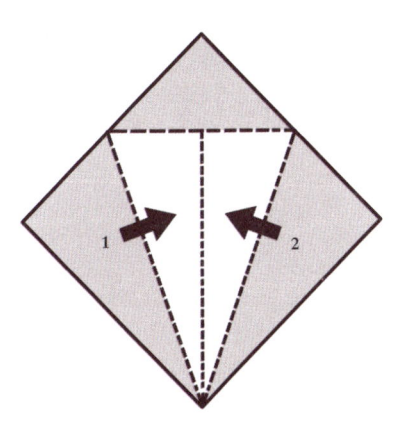

b. Fold over the top corner *(3)*.

c. Fold up the front corner *(4)*.

2. Remove the soiled nappy
With the baby lying on its back on a soft changing mat or comfortable towel, unpin the soiled nappy and remove, using it to wipe away any poo. Place the soiled nappy in a nappy bucket filled with water where it can soak until you are ready to put it into the wash.

3. Clean the baby
Using a baby wipe, and holding the baby's legs up, clean the baby's bottom thoroughly, wiping from front to back.

4. Secure the clean nappy
Position the clean, folded nappy under the baby, bringing the front portion up between the baby's legs and the side flaps round to the front. With your free hand between your baby's skin and the fabric, insert the safety pin, taking care not to push it through all the inner layers of towelling.

5. Check the final fit
The nappy should fit snugly but not so tight as to pinch the baby's skin. A waterproof nappy cover or wrap can be used over the terry nappy for extra protection.

TIP
★

To avoid pricking the baby with safety pins, secure the nappy using a 'nappi nippa' – a plastic device with hooks that grab the terry towelling in three places.

WARNING

★

Beware being sprayed by a baby boy.

IDENTIFY STRENGTHS AND AREAS FOR IMPROVEMENT

★

Tick the correct score bubble:

	bad	fair	good	very good	excellent
Nappy folding	0 1	2 3 4	5 6	7 8	9 10
Baby cleaning	0 1	2 3 4	5 6	7 8	9 10
General fit	0 1	2 3 4	5 6	7 8	9 10
Leakage test	0 1	2 3 4	5 6	7 8	9 10

Total score ——— **Evaluator** ———

Score: ★★★ 33–40 / ★★ 17–32.99 / ★ 5–16.99 / Call your mother 0–4.99

WEEK 45

SHARPENING A CARVING KNIFE

★

A blunt knife can ruin efforts at carving a turkey. It is also more likely to cause injury than a sharp knife because of the extra force required to make a cut. The aim of this task is to produce a razor sharp edge to your carving knife, without doing injury to yourself, or anyone else.

You will need: blunt carving knife, sharpening stone, sharpening steel, eye protection, well lit room with workbench, butcher's cap (optional)

TECHNIQUE

1. Select a good knife
Make sure you choose a good quality knife with a steel or carbon steel blade and a comfortable handle.

2. Find an appropriate place to sharpen your knife
You need a stable surface in a well lit room, away from food that might be contaminated by loose metal particles from the blade. Wear protective eye goggles.

3. Sharpen the knife using a sharpening stone
Most sharpening stones are 'wetstones', made of natural stone, which require a coating of oil or water before and during use. Choose one with both a rough and a fine side. If the knife is very blunt, start by passing it over the rough side, then finish on the fine side. Keep the knife at a 15-20 degree angle to the stone and draw the full length of the blade over the abrasive surface several times in the same direction, using light, even strokes, the same number on each side of the blade *(a)*.

a. Pass the knife over the sharpening stone at a 15-20 degree angle.

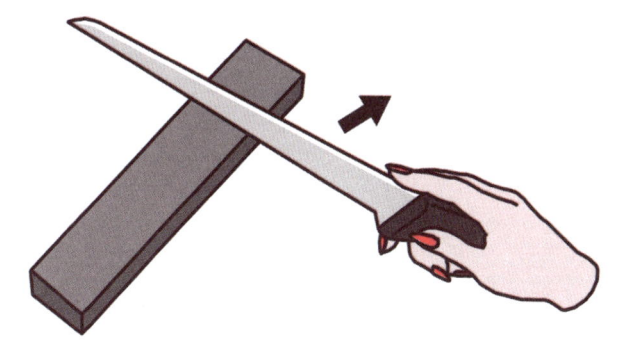

b. Draw the knife blade along the steel.

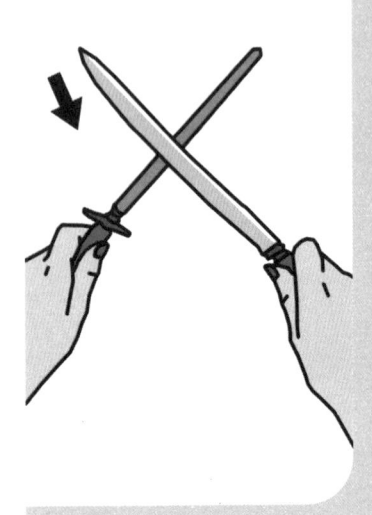

4. Hone the knife edge with a sharpening steel

Use a traditional butcher's steel, a round rod with protected handle, to smooth off the knife's surface after sharpening and to maintain the sharpened edge. Holding the steel in one hand with the tip pointing upwards, use the other to draw the full length of the knife blade smoothly and gently along the steel, keeping the angle at 15-20 degrees *(b)*. Repeat 10-20 times, alternating with both sides of the knife and steel to hone the knife blade on both edges. Start slowly and be careful because the knife will be extremely sharp.

5. Test the knife

The sharpness of the knife can be tested on a piece of paper, which should easily slice into ribbons with a sharp knife.

6. Use the steel to maintain the sharp edge

Each time you use the knife, hone the blade on the sharpening steel to maintain the cutting edge. If the steel is used regularly, you will rarely need to use the sharpening stone.

IF ALL THIS MAKES YOU NERVOUS
★
- Buy an electric knife sharpener. • Send the knife to a professional grinder.

SAFETY ADVICE

★

Don't play with knives.

PERFORMANCE ASSESSMENT

★

Cut finger	**0 points**
Massacred roast	**1 point**
Sharpened knife and stylishly carved turkey	**25 points**

WEEK 46

SHAMPOOING A DOG

★

Washing a dog's coat too often can remove essential protective oils so find a dog that hasn't been washed for a very long time. To avoid mess, wear waterproof clothing, collect the equipment you need before you begin, and keep the dog calm. When finished the dog's coat should look shiny and smell fresh. Remember to dry the dog before letting it go.

You will need: dirty dog, dog shampoo, dog brush and comb, dog towels, hairdryer (optional), bathtub, rubber shower mat, sponge, plastic container, waterproof clothing

TECHNIQUE

1. Preparation
Groom the dog outside, brushing off dried mud and untangling knotted hair. Collect everything you need and put it in the bathroom. Place the shower mat and an old towel in the bathtub to stop the dog from scratching the enamel.

2. Run the water
The water should be warm and not too hot. Run just a few inches (about 10 cm) and then lift the dog into the bathtub.

3. Wet the dog all over
Using a plastic container, scoop small amounts of water over the dog, thoroughly wetting the hair from the head downwards *(a)*. Avoid pouring water inside the ears, and use a sponge on the face and other delicate areas.

4. Shampoo the dog
Apply a small amount of dog shampoo (ask the vet which type is appropriate for the dog or for removing a particular odour). Work it into the coat, from head downwards *(b)*. Be careful not to get shampoo into the dog's eyes.

a. Thoroughly wet the dog's hair from its head downwards.

5. Rinse the dog thoroughly
Begin rinsing the coat from head downwards. Drain off the water in the bathtub and run some more at the same temperature and to the same depth. Continue rinsing until all soap has gone.

6. Dry the dog
Run off the final rinse water. Let the dog shake while it is in the bathtub, and use a towel to dry off excess water. Lift the dog out and dry thoroughly with towels. If using a hairdryer, keep it on low heat, at least 6 inches (15 cm) from the dog's coat *(c)*. When dry, groom the dog with a clean brush.

b. Work the shampoo into the coat.

c. Keep the hairdryer at least 6 inches (15 cm) from the dog's coat.

TIP
★

Don't let go of the dog prematurely.

WARNING
★

Washing-up liquid is not a recommended dog shampoo.

FOR HIGH FLYERS
★

Wash and blow-dry an Afghan hound.

IDENTIFY STRENGTHS AND AREAS FOR IMPROVEMENT
★

Tick the correct score bubble:

After 15 minutes	bad	fair	good	very good	excellent
Appearance of dog	0 1	2 3 4	5 6	7 8	9 10
Appearance of walls	0 1	2 3 4	5 6	7 8	9 10
Appearance of floors	0 1	2 3 4	5 6	7 8	9 10
Appearance of handler	0 1	2 3 4	5 6	7 8	9 10

Total score _____ **Evaluator** _____

Score: ★★★ 33–40 / ★★ 17–32.99 / ★ 5–16.99 / Don't try again 0–4.99

WEEK 47

MAKING FRIENDS IN THE OFFICE

★

Choose an office where you do not already have friends. You will need to chat to people and offer them drinks, cakes, chocolates and birthday or get well cards. Make an effort to circulate and do not leave anyone out – the more popular you are the more friends you will make. Be prepared to discuss office politics. Keep high standards of grooming and personal hygiene at all times.

You will need: work colleagues, doughnuts, cakes, biscuits, chocolates, strawberries, ice creams, birthday cards

TECHNIQUE

1. Identify the most friendly people
Target people who are open and friendly. If you can become their friends first you will have a greater chance befriending others who are less forthcoming.

2. Have something interesting to say
It is not sufficient to say 'hello'. You must also ask how they are and listen to their response. Make relevant and interesting points when they have finished talking.

3. Keep a bowl of sweets on your desk
Make sure you have a regular supply of sweets, cakes or doughnuts on your desk, together with strawberries or other low-fat alternatives. Bring in extra on special festival days and let everyone know by email.

a. Shy colleagues will appreciate a personal visit.

4. For shy colleagues
Take the goodies round and offer them personally *(a)*. A shy colleague will appreciate this gesture and may even become a life-long friend.

5. Remember birthdays
Keep a diary with everyone's birthdays. Buy them a card and bake a cake. If they are ill, visit them in hospital.

6. Organise a social event
Invite everyone to a party. Give out the invitations personally *(b)*. Hang around the tearoom and photocopier where your colleagues congregate and try and find out people's preferences. Then plan your party with the right drink, music and atmosphere to keep everyone happy.

b. Invite your work colleagues to a party.

TIP
★
Avoid spending all your salary on treats.

WARNING
★
Don't leave anyone out, especially your boss.

IDENTIFY STRENGTHS AND AREAS FOR IMPROVEMENT
★
After one week:

You discover no one likes doughnuts	0 points
You get fired for keeping an untidy desk	5 points
You are referred to a psychiatrist	5 points
Everyone comes to your party	20 points

Total score

WEEK 48

DEODORIZING A REFRIGERATOR

★

A refrigerator rapidly acquires an unpleasant mix of odours when fish and dairy products, meat, vegetables and cat food are stored together. If left too long, it can become a health hazard. Aim to thoroughly cleanse and deodorize a refrigerator that hasn't been cleaned for six months. You will need rubber gloves for protection.

You will need: smelly fridge, rubber gloves, bicarbonate of soda, activated charcoal, metal trays, anti-bacterial cleaning solution, sponges

TECHNIQUE

1. Empty the fridge
Turn the power off and transfer food to a cool place. Throw out any decomposing items. Remove shelves, trays, racks and food boxes from inside the fridge.

2. Clean inside and out
Using an anti-bacterial spray, a sponge and warm water, clean all surfaces, including the rubber door gasket. Wash the drip tray, shelves, racks and food boxes in the sink. Follow your refrigerator operating instructions for removing and cleaning the drain pan (below the refrigerator).

3. Wash the inside using a baking soda solution
Baking soda helps to neutralize odours. Make a baking soda solution (1 tablespoon of baking soda in 2 pints [1 litre] of hot water) and rewash all interior surfaces. Then rinse everything using a clean sponge. Leave the fridge door open for at least 20 minutes to allow to dry. Replace shelves, trays, etc, and turn the power back on.

4. Leave baking soda inside the fridge
If the fridge is still smelly, put some baking soda into a bowl and leave the bowl in the fridge for 24 hours, then discard. Food can be left in the fridge during this time.

5. Leave activated charcoal inside the fridge
For persistent odours, buy activated charcoal from a hardware store or appliance service company and leave on metal trays inside the fridge for 10 hours. The charcoal will absorb smells. It can be reactivated and used again by heating in a moderate oven for 30 minutes.

6. Prevent future odours
To prevent odours building up in future, keep an open box of baking soda in the fridge and replace every two months.

FOR HIGH FLYERS

★

Learn to spot mould, bacteria and mildew.

IDENTIFY STRENGTHS AND AREAS FOR IMPROVEMENT

★

Get an aunt to give an honest assessment:

	bad	fair	good	very good	excellent
Removal of decomposing food	0 1	2 3 4	5 6	7 8	9 10
Removal of smell	0 1	2 3 4	5 6	7 8	9 10
Use of airtight containers	0 1	2 3 4	5 6	7 8	9 10
Sparkle factor	0 1	2 3 4	5 6	7 8	9 10

Total score _____   **Evaluator** _____

Score: ★★★ 33–40 / ★★ 17–32.99 / ★ 5–16.99 / Try harder 0–4.99

WEEK 49

MAKING A PAPER AEROPLANE

★

There are many situations when you may need to make a paper aeroplane. For example, to demonstrate the phenomenon of lift produced by the action of air underneath a flat paper surface. The objective of this task is to produce a well balanced paper aeroplane that flies reliably and accurately in a horizontal position for as long and far as possible.

You will need: sheet of A4 paper

TECHNIQUE

1. Making the aeroplane
a) Fold the paper in half lengthways.
b) Open it out again and fold over the top corners of each side.
c) Fold the pointed end over, turning it backwards and forwards three times to create a concertina fold. The extra weight of this fold at the front of the aeroplane will help the plane to fly straight.
d) Fold the top corners over again.
e) Fold the sides back along the centrefold to form the point at the front of the aeroplane.
f) Fold down the top wings in a straight diagonal line beginning at the pointed front.
g) Fold over half-inch (10 mm) 'winglets' at the side of each wing.

2. Launching the aeroplane
Pinch the nose of the aeroplane to make sure the point is straight, then holding the plane underneath between thumb and first finger launch it gently into the air in a smooth, horizontal movement.

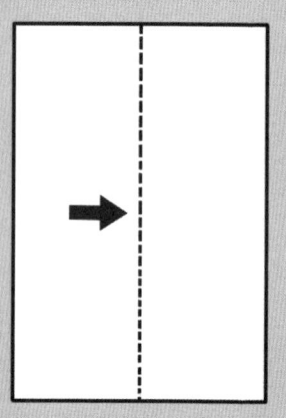

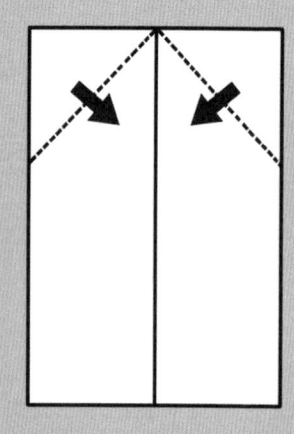

c.

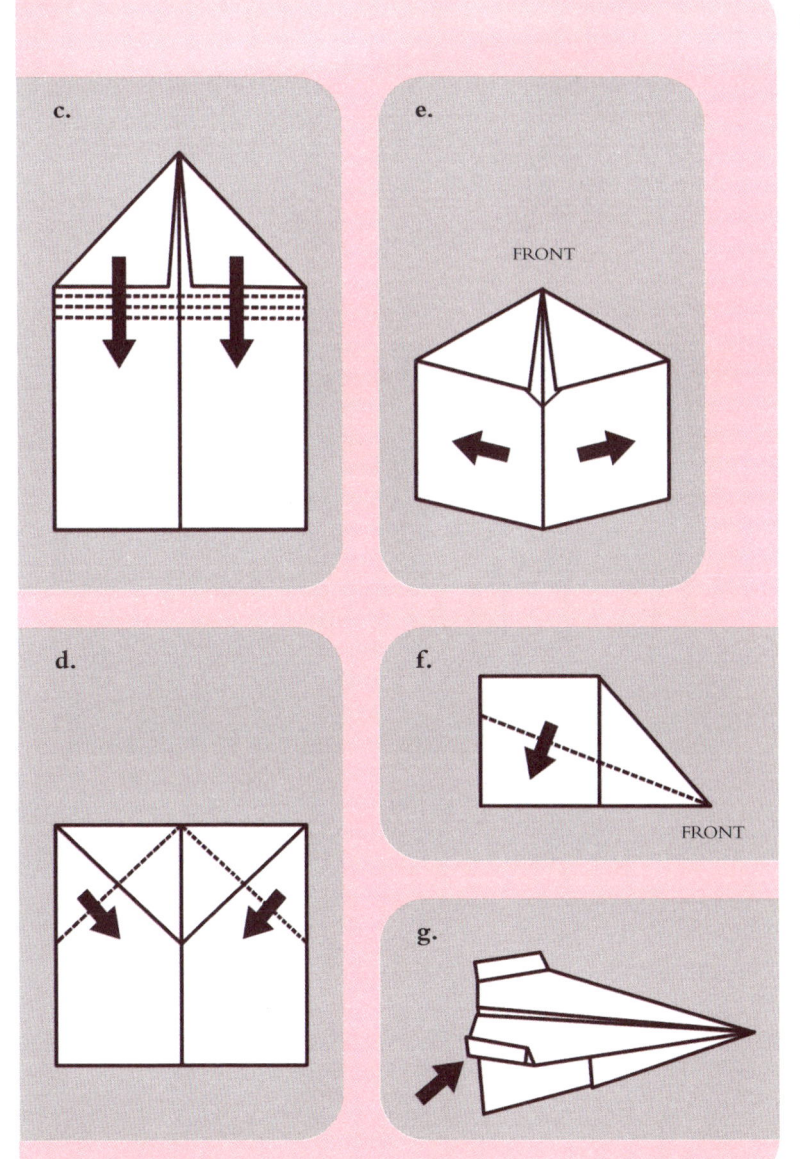

d.

e. FRONT

f. FRONT

g.

PERFORMANCE INDICATOR

★

An aeroplane that flies more than 65 feet (20 m) on level ground is exceptional.

FOR HIGH FLYERS

★

Make a paper aeroplane out of fluorescent paper and fly it at night.

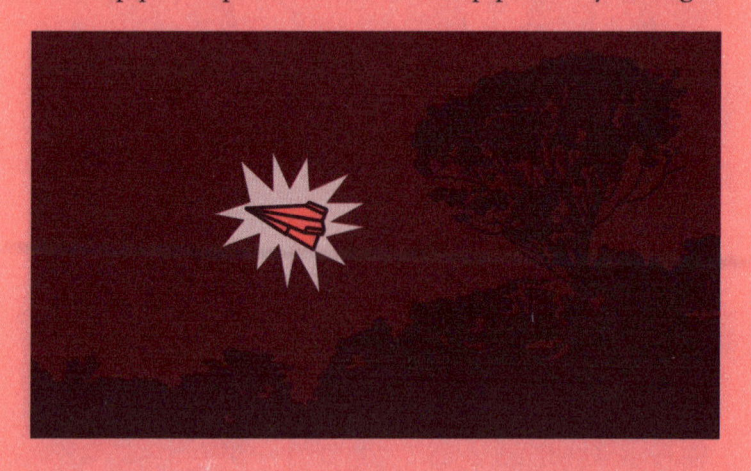

IDENTIFY STRENGTHS AND AREAS FOR IMPROVEMENT

★

Distance flown on level ground	Less than 16 feet (5 m)	**5 points**
	Between 16 and 32 feet (5–10 m)	**10 points**
	Over 32 feet (10 m)	**15 points**
Time aeroplane is in the air	Less than 3 seconds	**5 points**
	Anything above this	**15 points**
Mean angle of deviation from target	More than 90 degrees	**2 points**
	Less than 20 degrees	**15 points**
	Anything in-between	**5 points**
Total score		

WEEK 50

MENDING A FUSE IN THE DARK

★

A fuse melts if too much electricity passes through it and is a protection against more dangerous overheating. It can blow at any time but try this task when least convenient – at night. The broken fuse may only cut your plug circuit, leaving your overhead lights intact, or it may cut a lighting circuit. In either event, turn the power off at the mains before you start.

You will need: blown fuse, darkness, torch, fuse wire or replacement cartridge fuse

TECHNIQUE

1. Switch off all lights/appliances
Determine which circuit has blown – the plug circuit or a lighting circuit. Turn off all lights/appliances on the faulty circuit.

2. Locate the fuse box
Find the box containing the fuses for all electrical circuits in the house. Switch off the mains switch before starting work. Get someone to hold a torch or rig up an alternative light source.

3. Repairing a rewirable fuse
Pull out each of the rectangular fuseholders from the fuse box, one at a time. If they are of the rewirable type, check which one has a melted wire. Remove the remains of the broken fuse wire and replace with fuse wire of an appropriate rating (thickness) for the fuse (depending on circuit design, the rating for a plug circuit fuse could be either 20 or 30 amps; a lighting circuit fuse is normally 5 amps). Wind the wire around the terminals at each end of the fuseholder and trim the excess *(a)*. The wire should not be pulled taut.

a. Replace the fuse wire in a rewirable fuse.

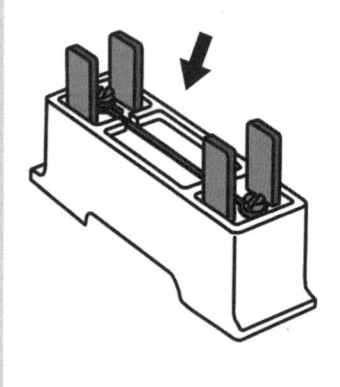

4. Replacing a cartridge fuse
A cartridge fuse though simpler to change is less obvious to see when it has blown. The fuse wire

is enclosed in a ceramic cartridge with metal ends, which fits into clips in the fuseholder (like the fuses inside plugs). If you do not have a continuity tester to check the fuse, try a replacement fuse of the correct rating and see if it restores the circuit when the mains is switched on *(b)*. Check each fuse in turn until you find one that has blown.

5. Restore the mains supply and test lights/appliances
Turn the supply back on. Switch on each appliance/light one by one, noting, if the fuse blows again, which one is the cause (the cause may be an appliance with a damaged flex or too many appliances connected to one circuit). If you cannot identify the fault, and the problem persists, call an electrician.

b. Replace the cartridge in a cartridge fuse.

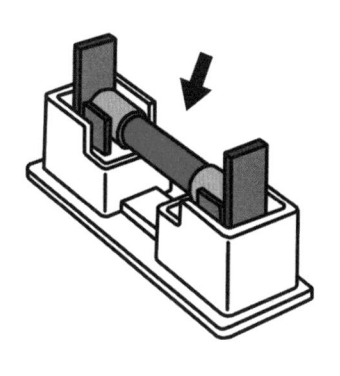

6. If you have a miniature circuit breaker
If you find a miniature circuit breaker inside your fuse box, the switch inside it will have tripped (turning off the mains) and protected the fuses in the fuse box from blowing. Try resetting the trip switch. If the fault that tripped it off is still present it will not allow you to reset. You will first need to find the appliance or other fault that caused the switch to trip.

ALTERNATIVE APPROACH

★

If your electrics blow at night, go to bed early.

WARNING

★

Electricity can kill. If in doubt, call a qualified electrician.

DON'T CONFUSE

★

A power cut to homes in your area with an electrical fault in your house.

IDENTIFY STRENGTHS AND AREAS FOR IMPROVEMENT

★

Tick the correct score bubble:

	bad	fair	good	very good	excellent
Finding fuse box	0 1	2 3 4	5 6	7 8	9 10
Repairing fuse	0 1	2 3 4	5 6	7 8	9 10
Identifying fault	0 1	2 3 4	5 6	7 8	9 10
Avoiding injury	0 1	2 3 4	5 6	7 8	9 10

Total score ———— **Evaluator** ————

Score: ★★★ 33–40 / ★★ 17–32.99 / ★ 5–16.99 / Call an electrician 0–4.99

WEEK 51

PRESERVING A CHRISTMAS TREE

★

Practise this task at Christmas time when you have a Christmas tree and a good reason to preserve it. Treat your tree with care and attention and it will survive inside the house throughout the festive season, and much longer outside if it's a living tree with a rootball attached. Measure your success in terms of how quickly the needles fall off.

You will need: Christmas tree, large waterproof container, water

TECHNIQUE

1. Select a good tree
For cut trees, check for freshness by gently feeling or shaking the branches. Avoid trees with dead growth or where the green pine needles drop easily to the ground. For living, root-balled trees, make sure the rootball is large and undisturbed.

2. The journey home
Try not to squash the tree on the journey home. When handling a living tree, pick it up by the rootball and not by the stem or branches.

3. On arrival
Once home, cut an inch (2.5 cm) from the base of the cut tree and place the tree in a large bucket of tap water in a cool and protected area, for example in the garage. The new cut allows the tree to take in water – up to a gallon (4.5 litres) during the first 24 hours. For a root-balled tree, keep the rootball moist.

4. After a couple of days, move the tree indoors
Once the tree has acclimatised to the garage environment, move it indoors. Find a cool position, away from heaters and direct sunlight.

5. Erect and look after the tree
Erect the cut tree on a firm stand incorporating a waterproof container, which should be topped up with water every day. The living tree planted indoors will also need regular watering. Switch off decorative tree lights at night or when you leave the house – hot bulbs can ignite a fire as the tree gradually dries out.

6. After Christmas
Plant the living tree outside in a sheltered spot as soon as the ground thaws, using plenty of compost and leaf mulch around the ball. Recycle a cut tree, for example, get it chipped for your flower beds or cut the branches and store until dry enough to use for fuel.

ALTERNATIVELY

★

Buy a fibre-optic, special effect tree with colours to match your décor.

TIP

★

Do not use a garden sprinkler to water your tree.

PERFORMANCE ASSESSMENT

★

Fill in the correct score:
poor: 0/1   fair: 2/3/4   good: 5/6   very good: 7/8   excellent: 9/10

	Day 1	Day 2	Day 3	Day 4	Day 5	Day 6	Day 7	Day 8	Day 9
Needle retention									

Total Christmas score _____   (70+ points: 2 helpings of Christmas pudding)

WEEK 52

GETTING GUESTS TO GO HOME

★

Part of running a successful party involves making sure your guests go home at the appropriate time. The correct approach is to get visitors to leave voluntarily and without feeling they have outstayed their welcome, even if they have. To succeed you must make it clear when the party is supposed to end, and remain respectful and polite if things get sticky.

You will need: reluctant-to-go-home guests, dog or baby

TECHNIQUE

1. Send out party invitations
Include on the invitation the beginning and end times for the party. Use words like 'The party will begin promptly at 7.30 p.m. and end at 11.00 p.m.' Some of your guests will arrange pick-ups or taxis to take them home, at which stage the others (if polite) will be reminded that they should go too.

2. Remove the alcohol
About one hour before the end of the party, remove all remaining full bottles of alcohol and serve strong, hot coffee.

3. Turn the lights up and the heating off
Put on some bright lights and – for a winter party – chill the room with an open window and heat turned off.

4. Let loose the dog or a baby
If you have a dog, preferably a big one with a long tongue who has been locked in a room all night, now is the time to let it run round licking the guests *(a)*. A small baby handed to each guest in turn will do as an alternative.

5. Make a leaving speech
Thank people for coming and say how much you have enjoyed their company. Explain that mints are served, that you are sure everyone is tired and keen to go home, and that you have a telephone number for the taxi rank if anyone needs it.

6. Last resort
For persistent over-stayers, say you've got a long day ahead and are sorry but you will have to go to bed. Ask them to put the cat out when they leave.

a. Let your dog loose to lick the guests.

FOR GUESTS WHO DON'T KNOW WHEN TO LEAVE

★

• Start the washing up. • Suggest a game of charades. • Get out your holiday snaps. • Go to sleep in a chair and snore loudly. • Don't invite them next time.

WARNING

★

Persistent late-stayers sometimes enjoy looking at holiday snaps.

IDENTIFY STRENGTHS AND AREAS FOR IMPROVEMENT

★

Ask your guests to give an honest assessment:

	bad	fair	good	very good	excellent
Politeness	0 1	2 3 4	5 6	7 8	9 10
Subtlety	0 1	2 3 4	5 6	7 8	9 10
Effectiveness	0 1	2 3 4	5 6	7 8	9 10
Total score	**Evaluator**				

Score: ★★★ 25–30 / ★★ 19–24.99 / ★ 4–18.99 / Try a new approach 0–3.99

ABOUT THE AUTHORS

★

Nicola Chalton is a freelance writer and editor living in London. She sleeps in a bed with hospital corners surrounded by her rapidly expanding snowdome collection.

Pascal Thivillon is a designer and illustrator. He has published two cartoon books about the joys of everyday life. His ambition is to make a space rocket mobile.

ACKNOWLEDGEMENTS

★

The authors would like to thank all the friends, family, colleagues, experts and casual acquaintances who have kindly passed on tips, information and advice in the compilation of this book. In particular, we will mention by name Global Shakeup/Snowdomes for information on snowdome collecting, Beds & Herts Hedgehog Rescue for hedgehog advice and Martina Habeck for excellent tips on eradicating slugs and snails.

OTHER REAL*LIFE* GUIDES SOON AVAILABLE

★

The Social Status Handbook
How to behave according to your class.

The Idleness Handbook
How to achieve the difficult art of doing nothing.

The Urban Life Handbook
How to survive in a big city.

The Rural Life Handbook
How to survive the countryside.

The Hobo's Handbook
How to make the vagrant lifestyle work for you.

The Pensioner's Handbook
How to enjoy life when you're getting on a bit.

★

Basement Press would be pleased to receive feedback on this book and any ideas for future Real*life* guides. Please write to: info@basementpress.com